# MANTER'S
# ESSENTIALS OF
# CLINICAL
# NEUROANATOMY and
# NEUROPHYSIOLOGY

## ARTHUR J. GATZ, Ph.D.

*Professor of Anatomy, Medical College of Georgia*

## 4th EDITION

F. A. DAVIS *Company*

PHILADELPHIA

*Second printing, September 1970*

*Third printing, April 1971*

*Fourth printing, January 1972*

*Fifth printing, September 1972*

Library of Congress Catalog Card Number 70-103536

ISBN-0-8036-3940-6

# Preface to the Fourth Edition

It has been my intention to preserve the objectives of the late Dr. Manter which are stated in his preface.

.A number of revisions have been made throughout the book. The material on the auditory and autonomic nervous systems has been entirely rewritten. Four of the diagrams have been improved. A sincere effort has been made to up-date the information in the text.

I am grateful to Mr. Steve Harrison for his efforts on four of the diagrams in this edition.

Arthur J. Gatz

# Preface to the First Edition

This book has been written with the object of providing a short, but comprehensive survey of the human nervous system. It is hoped that it will furnish a unified concept of structure and function which will be of practical value in leading to the understanding of the working mechanisms of the brain and spinal cord. Neither of these two aspects—structure and function—stands apart from the other. Together they furnish the key to the significance of the abnormal changes in function that go hand in hand with structural lesions of the nervous system. The viewpoints of three closely dependent sciences—neuroanatomy, neurophysiology and clinical neurology—are combined and used freely, not with the intent of covering these fields exhaustively, but in the belief that a more discerning approach to the study of the nervous system can be attained by bringing together all three facets of the subject.

To suit the needs of the medical student, or the physician who wishes to review the nervous system efficiently, basic information is presented in concise form. Consequently, it has not been feasible to cite published reports of research from which present concepts of the nervous system have evolved. The planning and arrangement of the chapters are such that whole topics can be covered rapidly. Presenting the subject material to classes in this form allows more time for discussion and review, or, if the teacher desires, for lectures dealing with advanced aspects, than would otherwise be permitted.

For the encouragement and valuable suggestions they have given me, I am indebted to my former colleague, Dr. William H. Waller, Jr., and to Dr. Lester L. Bowles. I am deeply grateful to Mr. A. H. Germagian for executing most of the drawings and diagrams, and to Mr. Richard Meyers for his special assistance with the illustrations.

JOHN T. MANTER

# Contents

## CHAPTER 7

Lesions of Peripheral Nerves. Lesions of the Posterior Roots. Lesions of the Anterior Horns. Lesions of the Central Gray Matter. Lesions Involving Both the Anterior Horns and the Pyramidal Tracts. Lesions Involving Both the Posterior and the Lateral Funiculi. Thrombosis of the Anterior Spinal Artery. Hemisection of the Spinal Cord. Tumors of the Spinal Cord. Degenerative Changes in Nerve Cells. Regeneration of Nerve Fibers.

## CHAPTER 8

Medulla. External Markings of the Medulla. Internal Structures of the Medulla. Pons. External Markings of the Pons. Internal Structure of the Pons. Midbrain. External Markings of the Midbrain. Internal Structures of the Midbrain.

## CHAPTER 9

Résumé of Functional Components. The Anatomical Position of Cranial Nerve Nuclei in the Brain Stem. An Outline of the Functional Components in the Cranial Nerves.

## CHAPTER 10

The Hypoglossal Nerve. The Accessory Nerve. The Vagus Nerve Complex. Course and Distribution of the Nerves of the Vagal System. The Motor Portion of the Vagal System. The Parasympathetic Portion of the Vagal System. The Sensory Portion of the Vagal System. Reflexes of the Vagal System.

## CHAPTER 11

The Abducent Nerve. The Trochlear Nerve. The Oculomotor Nerve. The Facial Nerve. The Trigeminal Nerve.

## CHAPTER 12

The Auditory System. The Auditory Pathway. Bilateral Representation of the Ears in Each Temporal Lobe. Hearing Defects from Nerve Damage and from Mechanical Obstruction. Auditory Reflexes.

CHAPTER 13

The Vestibular Nerve and Its Central Connections. The Vestibulospinal Tracts. The Vestibulomesencephalic Tract. Vestibular Nystagmus. Sensory Aspects of Vestibular Stimulation.

CHAPTER 14

Primary Subdivisions of the Cerebellum. The Peduncles of the Cerebellum. The Synergistic Function of the Cerebellum. Afferent and Efferent Pathways of the Cerebellum. Feed-Back Circuits Through the Cerebellum. Clinical Signs of Cerebellar Dysfunction.

CHAPTER 15

Lesions of the Basal Part of the Medulla. Lesions of the Central Region of the Upper Medulla. Lesions of the Dorsolateral Region of the Upper Medulla. Lesions of the Basal Portion of the Caudal Part of the Pons. Lesions of the Pontocerebellar Angle. Lesions of the Middle Region of the Pons. Lesions of the Basal Part of the Midbrain. Lesions of the Tegmentum of the Midbrain. Lesions of the Superior Colliculi.

CHAPTER 16

The Visual Pathway. Effects of Lesions Interrupting the Visual Pathway.

CHAPTER 17

The Light Reflex. Reflexes Associated with the Near-Point Reaction. The Argyll Robertson Pupil. The Visual Fixation Reflex. Protective Reflexes. The Pain Reflex.

CHAPTER 18

Divisions of the Autonomic Nervous System. The Sympathetic Nervous System Division. The Sympathetic Innervation of the Adrenal Gland. The Parasympathetic Nervous System. The Innervation of the Urinary Bladder.

## CHAPTER 1

# Introduction

## Nerve Cells and Nerve Fibers

The *neuron* (nerve cell) is the functional and anatomical unit of the nervous system. Each consists of a *cell body* (*cyton*) and one to several dozen processes of varying length called *nerve fibers*. *Dendrites* are short branching fibers which normally receive impulses at their peripheral terminals and conduct them toward the nerve cell body. The term *axon*, in a strict sense, applies to a single long fiber conducting impulses away from a nerve cell body. Any long fiber, however, is commonly called an axon regardless of the direction of conduction.

Nerve cell bodies are usually located in groups. Outside the brain and spinal cord such groups are called *ganglia*. In the cortex of the cerebrum and cerebellum nerve cells are arranged in very extensive laminated sheets. Elsewhere within the brain and spinal cord they form groups of various sizes and shapes known as *nuclei*. In this instance the term *nucleus* has a different meaning from the nucleus of an individual cell. Those regions of the brain and cord which contain aggregations of nerve cell bodies comprise the *gray matter*, and in the fresh state, they are grayish in color. The remaining areas consist primarily of myelinated nerve fibers and make up the *white matter*.

Some nerve fibers are naked axis cylinders, but most of them are encased in some sort of sheath. The majority of peripheral nerve fibers have a *myelin sheath* and a *neurilemma* (*sheath of Schwann*) as well. Peripheral autonomic fibers (postganglionic) have no myelin sheath but retain a neurilemma. Fibers which are located in the white matter of the brain and spinal cord possess a myelin sheath but have no neurilemma.

Nerve fibers of the brain and spinal cord which have a common origin and a common destination constitute a *tract*. Although a tract occupies a regular position, it does not always form a compact bundle because of some dispersion with intermingling fibers of neighboring tracts. There are a number of bundles of fibers in the brain which are so distinct anatomically that they have been given the names *fasciculus, brachium, peduncle, column,* or *lemniscus*. These may contain only a single tract, or they may comprise several running together in the same bundle. *Nerve, nerve root, nerve trunk, nerve cord,* and *ramus* are appropriate anatomical terms for bundles of nerve fibers outside the brain and spinal cord.

Transmission of impulses from neuron to neuron occurs at a *synapse* —a place where fine branches of one neuron are in contact with the cell body or processes of another neuron. Synaptic ramifications of dendrites

1

and terminal branches of axons form a delicate network throughout the gray substance known as *neuropil*. Nerve cells are normally stimulated at only one set of terminals and thus conduct impulses in only one direction, away from the region which receives stimulation. *Afferent fibers* (dendrites) conduct the impulse toward the cell body; *efferent fibers* conduct away from the cell body. The fibers of the dorsal roots of the spinal cord, for example, are spinal afferents. It is customary to name fibers by formulating a compound word which contains the name of their place of origin followed by the name of their termination. For example, thalamocortical fibers go from the thalamus to the cerebral cortex.

## The Peripheral Nervous System

The cranial and spinal nerves with their associated ganglia make up the peripheral nervous system. Motor fibers of peripheral nerves are of two types: *somatic motor fibers* which terminate in skeletal muscle, and *autonomic fibers* which furnish innervation to cardiac muscle, smooth muscle and glands. The *sensory fibers* of nerves receive stimuli from receptor end organs of various types. Each fiber conducts impulses toward the spinal cord and brain from the particular receptor with which it is connected.

## The Central Nervous System

The central nervous system (CNS) consists of the brain and the spinal cord. The brain of the young adult male averages 1380 grams in weight (generally 100 grams less in females). The brain is generally divided into three regions, the cerebrum, the brain stem and the cerebellum.

### The Cerebrum

The two cerebral hemispheres are incompletely separated by a deep, *medial longitudinal fissure*. They are joined together at the bottom of this fissure by the *corpus callosum*, a broad band of commissural fibers. The surface of each hemisphere is wrinkled by the presence of eminences known as *gyri* and furrows which are called *sulci*, or *fissures*. The fissures are deeper and can be recognized internally by corresponding indentations of the ventricles of the brain. A layer of cerebral cortex 1.3 to 4.5 mm. thick covers the expansive surface of the cerebrum. It is estimated to contain 14,000,000,000 nerve cells.

There are two major grooves on the lateral surface of the brain. The *lateral fissure*, which begins as a deep cleft on the basal surface of the brain, extends laterally, posteriorly and upward (Fig. 1). The *central sulcus (of Rolando)* runs from the dorsal border of the hemisphere near its midpoint obliquely downward and forward until it nearly meets the lateral fissure. For descriptive purposes the hemisphere is divided into four lobes. The *frontal lobe* (approximately the anterior one-third of

2

the hemisphere) is the portion which is rostral to the central sulcus and above the lateral fissure. The *occipital lobe* is that part lying behind an arbitrary line drawn from the parieto-occipital fissure to the preoccipital notch. This lobe occupies a small area of the lateral surface but has more extensive territory on the medial aspect of the hemisphere. The *parietal lobe* extends from the central sulcus to the parieto-occipital fissure and is separated from the *temporal lobe* below by an imaginary line projected from the horizontal portion of the lateral fissure to the middle of the line demarking the occipital lobe. The gyri are subdivided areas roughly marked out by sulci whose patterns may show considerable individual variation.

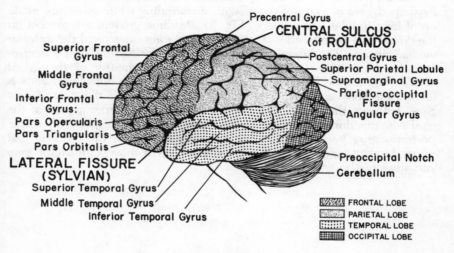

Fig. 1.   Lateral view of the brain.

## The Brain Stem

The brain stem consists of the following areas of the brain: medulla, pons, midbrain and diencephalon. This region is described in Chapter 8.

## The Spinal Cord

The spinal cord is a slender cylinder surrounded by the closely applied *pia mater*. A *dural sac* lined, on the inner surface, with the arachnoid membrane encloses a liberal amount of cerebrospinal fluid which occupies the *subarachnoid space*. The spinal cord is anchored to the dura by paired lateral septa of the pia—the *denticulate ligaments*. The cord is moderately enlarged in the cervical region and again in the lumbar region where nerve fibers supplying the upper and lower extremities are connected. Spinal nerves are attached to the cord in pairs: 8 cervical; 12 thoracic; 5 lumbar; 5 sacral; and 1 coccygeal. Each spinal nerve has dorsal and ventral roots which form nearly continuous rows along the cord. The spinal cord does not extend to the lower end of the vertebral

3

canal but ends at the level of the lower border of the first lumbar vertebra in a tapered cone, the *conus medullaris*. The pia matter continues caudally as a connective tissue filament, the *filum terminale*, attached to the periosteum of the coccyx. Since the cord is some 25 cm. shorter than the vertebral column, the lumbar and sacral nerves require very long roots extending from the cord to the intervertebral foramina where dorsal and ventral roots are joined. These roots descend in a bundle from the conus, and, from its resemblance to the tail of a horse, the formation is known as the *cauda equina*. Because of the difference in their lengths, the segments of the spinal cord are not aligned opposite corresponding segments of the vertebral column (Fig. 2).

In transverse section the spinal cord shows an H-shaped, or butterfly-shaped, area of gray substance with surrounding white substance made up of longitudinal nerve fibers (Fig. 3). Midline grooves are present on the dorsal and ventral sides—the *posterior median sulcus* and the *anterior median fissure*. The lateral surface contains a *dorsolateral* and a *ventrolateral sulcus*. These markings divide the white matter of the spinal cord into *posterior, lateral,* and *anterior funiculi*. The *dorsal root zone* is interposed between the posterior and lateral funiculi; the *ventral root zone,* between the lateral and anterior funiculi. The gray matter of the cord contains dorsal and ventral enlargements known respectively as the *posterior gray horns* and the *anterior gray horns*. In the thoracic and upper lumbar segments of the spinal cord small *intermediolateral gray columns* are also present.

4

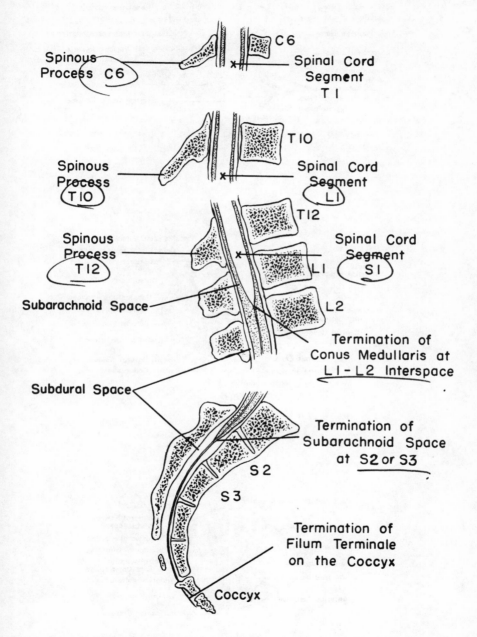

Spinous Process C6

Spinal Cord Segment T1

Spinous Process T10

Spinal Cord Segment L1

Spinous Process T12

Spinal Cord Segment S1

C6

T10

T12

L1

L2

S1

Subarachnoid Space

Subdural Space

Termination of Conus Medullaris at L1-L2 Interspace

Termination of Subarachnoid Space at S2 or S3

S2

S3

Termination of Filum Terminale on the Coccyx

Coccyx

Fig. 2. Diagram showing the relationship of certain structures of the spinal cord to the bodies and spinous processes of vertebrae.

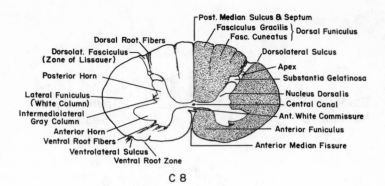

C 8

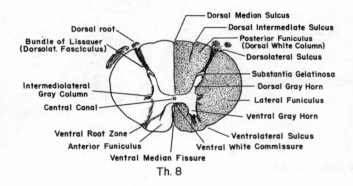

Th. 8

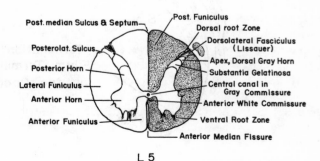

L 5

Fig. 3.   Cross sections of the spinal cord.

6

## CHAPTER 2

# The Voluntary Motor Pathway

All voluntary movements utilize nerve impulses conducted by long nerve fibers descending from the part of the cerebral cortex known as the *motor cortex*. Other areas may be responsible for the appropriate choice of movements to be performed, but the motor area is essential for their execution. If the motor cortex is destroyed, conscious effort is ineffective and paralysis results.

## The Motor Area of the Brain

The *motor area*—also known as Brodmann's area 4—is located in the *precentral* (or anterior central) *gyrus* of the frontal lobe. It forms a band extending from the lateral fissure upward to the dorsal border of the hemisphere and a short distance beyond on the medial surface of the frontal lobe. The left motor strip controls the right side of the body. The larynx and tongue are represented in the lowest part of this strip, followed in upward sequence by the face, thumb, hand, forearm, arm, thorax, abdomen, thigh, calf, foot, and the muscles of the perineum. In humans, areas for the hand, tongue and larynx are disproportionately large conforming with the development of elaborate motor control. The spatial organization of the motor cortex resembles a map showing a distorted image of the body turned upside down and reversed left for right (Fig. 4).

## Descending Fibers of the Motor Area

The *pyramidal system* consists of the descending fibers of the motor area of the brain; 3.5 to 4.0 per cent of these fibers come from gigantopyramidal cells (Betz cells) located in the fifth layer of cortical cells. Other supplementary sources are believed to exist in man. In the monkey, about one-third of the pyramidal fibers arise in area 4, one-third from area 6 (premotor area) and the remainder from the parietal lobe (primarily areas 1, 2 and 3). After crossing to the opposite side, pyramidal fibers are distributed to cells of voluntary motor nuclei of cranial nerves and to the motor cells of the anterior horns of the spinal cord. A short internuncial neuron probably completes the connection with the motor cell. The path over which impulses must travel from the motor cortex to striated muscles is generally considered to have two components:

1. Upper motor neurons (pyramidal fibers).
2. Lower motor neurons (peripheral nerve fibers).

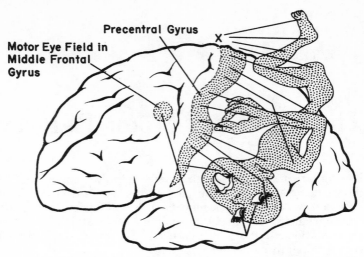

Fig. 4.   Manikin illustrating the topographic representation of the right side of the body in the motor area of the left frontal lobe.

### Corticospinal, Corticobulbar, and Corticomesencephalic Tracts

Upper motor neuron fibers may be divided, for convenience, into three groups (Fig. 5):

1. *Corticospinal Tract* (Pyramidal Tract Proper)

    This tract descends from the cerebral cortex to the spinal cord. The fibers, which are found in the white matter under the cortex, become grouped and then descend in the internal capsule, cerebral peduncle, pons, pyramid, pyramidal decussation and lateral cortico-spinal tract. A few fibers—variable in number—do not decussate and descend in the anterior funiculi of the spinal cord as the uncrossed *anterior pyramidal tracts*. The fibers of the anterior corticospinal tract decussate before they synapse with the lower motor neuron. This tract terminates in the cervical level of the cord. The *lateral corticospinal tract* occupies a position in the dorsal half of the lateral funiculus of the spinal cord. The number of fibers in the tract decreases in successively lower cord segments as more and more fibers reach their terminations.

2. *Corticobulbar Tract*  5, 7, 9, 10, 11, 12  X

    The fibers of the corticobulbar tract start out in company with the corticospinal tract but take a divergent route at the level of the midbrain. They terminate in the brain stem on voluntary motor nuclei of cranial nerves V (*trigeminal*); VII (*facial*); IX, X, and XI (*glossopharyngeal, vagus,* and *accessory*); and XII (*hypoglossal*). Most of them cross to the side opposite their origin, but uncrossed connections also exist.

3. *Corticomesencephalic Tract*  3, 4, 6  (Eye)(LR c SO 4) 3

    These are fibers descending to the nuclei of cranial nerves III (*oculomotor*), IV (*trochlear*), and VI (*abducent*) which furnish the motor supply to the extrinsic muscles of the eye. Corticomesencephalic

8

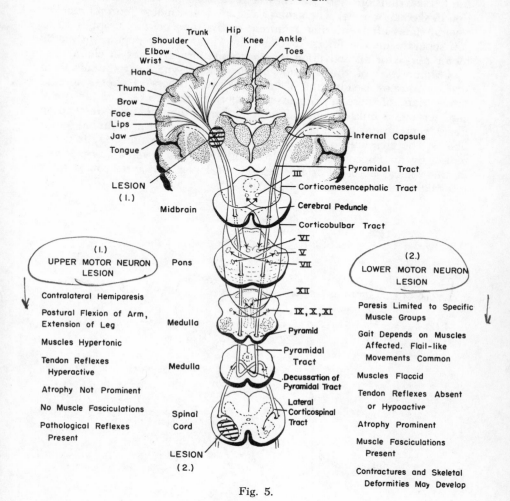

Fig. 5.

fibers do not arise from the motor area of the cortex but come from a separate cortical zone, area 8, rostral to it. Stimulation of this cortical area on the left causes both eyes to turn to the right. Many authorities include the corticomesencephalic tract with the cortico-bulbar.

## Lower Motor Neurons

Lower motor neurons are the conspicuously large cells located in the anterior horns of the spinal cord and in the motor nuclei of cranial nerves. The fibers take a ventrolateral course and emerge from the spinal cord in bundles which form the ventral roots. In company with dorsal root fibers they form spinal nerves and are distributed through the trunks, divisions and branches of peripheral nerves to their termination in skeletal muscle. The axon of a single lower motor neuron branches several times after entering a muscle so that one neuron supplies 10 to 300 separate muscle fibers. Skeletal muscle is totally dependent on its motor nerve for all activation whether voluntary or reflex in character.

Motor cells of the anterior horns receive synaptic terminals from several sources besides the voluntary control fibers of the pyramidal tract. Many of these are processes of short association cells of the spinal cord serving as links of reflex circuits. Others are terminals of descending fibers from various tracts collectively designated as extrapyramidal motor fibers. The character of a movement as it appears in the body is determined by an interplay of impulses impinging on lower motor neurons of the ventral horns. For this reason the lower motor neuron is often referred to as the "final common path."

Muscle tonus loss — if ventral root cut
Tonus of muscle loss — if dorsal root cut.

## CHAPTER 3

# The Stretch Reflex and Muscle Tonus

## Muscle Tonus

A normal, live muscle which appears to be fully relaxed still possesses a small amount of tension. If it is palpated in a resting state, the muscle will be found to have a quality of resilience rather than complete flabbiness. When it is passively stretched by moving one of the joints, a certain amount of resistance will be encountered in the muscle which is not related to any conscious effort on the part of the patient. These characteristics—subdued activity at rest, and involuntary reaction opposing mechanical stretch—are the chief clinical manifestations of muscle tonus.

A muscle loses its tonus at once if the ventral roots containing its motor nerve fibers are cut. Tonus is likewise abolished by cutting the dorsal nerve roots that contain the sensory fibers from the muscle. These familiar experiments indicate that tonus, of the sort that has been described, is maintained and regulated in muscles by reflex activity of the nervous system, and is not a property of isolated muscle.

## The Stretch Reflex

The stretch reflex is the basic neural mechanism for maintaining tonus in muscles. Aside from its role in keeping relaxed muscles slightly active, the stretch reflex is capable of increasing the tension of selected muscle groups to provide a background of postural muscle tonus on which voluntary movements are superimposed.

In any reflex, propagation of nerve impulses into the central nervous system over afferent fibers brings about a discharge of impulses over efferent fibers to effectors which produces a simple, appropriate action. Reflexes cannot operate successfully unless the proper synaptic connections between afferent and efferent fibers are established in the central nervous system. Most reflex arcs include at least one internuncial neuron between their afferent and efferent fibers. In this respect the stretch reflex is exceptional because its two fibers make direct synapse without any intermediary connecting neurons.

Stretching a muscle evokes a discharge of impulses in its neuromuscular spindles—specialized receptors that lie parallel with muscle fibers and interspersed between them. Afferent nerve fibers, whose peripheral terminals are spirally arranged about the intrafusal muscle fiber in the neuromuscular spindles, enter the spinal cord through a dorsal nerve root and turn ventrally across the gray matter of the spinal cord to reach the anterior horn (Fig. 6). At this point synapses with motor nerve cells

11

are effected. Axons of these lower motor neurons conduct impulses from the spinal cord to motor end-plates in muscle fibers which activate the fibers and produce increased tension in the muscle. Since the motor response takes place in the same muscle that is stimulated, the stretch reflex is essentially a mono-muscular reflex. The stimulation of the tendon receptors by excessive tension results in an inhibition of the motor neuron activity.

The status of a muscle's stretch reflex is usually tested by tapping its tendon to give it a slight, quick stretch. The reflex contraction that follows is commonly referred to as a deep reflex, or *tendon reflex*. For purposes of localization it is useful to know which segments of the spinal cord are concerned with specific tendon reflexes. The biceps brachii reflex, for example, utilizes cord segments C5–C6; the triceps brachii, C6–C7; the patellar tendon reflex, L2–L4; the triceps surae, L5–S2.

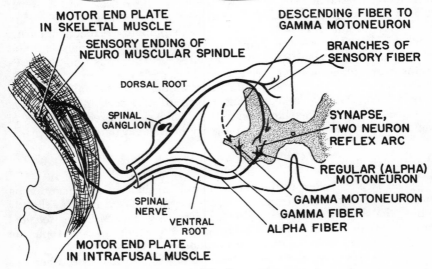

MOTOR END PLATE IN SKELETAL MUSCLE

DESCENDING FIBER TO GAMMA MOTONEURON

SENSORY ENDING OF NEURO MUSCULAR SPINDLE

BRANCHES OF SENSORY FIBER

DORSAL ROOT

SPINAL GANGLION

SYNAPSE, TWO NEURON REFLEX ARC

REGULAR (ALPHA) MOTONEURON

SPINAL NERVE

VENTRAL ROOT

GAMMA MOTONEURON

GAMMA FIBER

ALPHA FIBER

MOTOR END PLATE IN INTRAFUSAL MUSCLE

Fig. 6.

## Alpha and Gamma Motoneurons

The foregoing description of the myotatic (stretch) reflex is incomplete. Present knowledge indicates that the motor centers of the brain send impulses to skeletal muscle by two routes. One, well explained in older concepts, descends through intermediary units, generally, to the *alpha* or larger anterior horn cells. The other involves the *gamma* or small motoneuron (Fig. 6).

The gamma efferents cause contraction of the *intrafusal muscle fibers* within the *neuromuscular spindle*. The resulting increase in tonus of the intrafusal fibers within the spindle makes the muscle spindle more sensitive to stretch. Thus the amount of reflex tonus may be altered to fit varying circumstances. The minor change in tonus apparently is adequate to serve as a stimulus for the activation of the alpha motoneurons which control the reflex activity of the entire muscle mass.

12

It has been shown that the reticular formation has a regulatory control on the gamma efferent fibers. Stimulation of the "facilitory" reticular substance (in the mesencephalon and pons) augments the spindle discharge of the gamma fibers. This causes augmentation of myotatic reflex. Stimulation of the "inhibitory" reticular substance in the medulla (via the lateral reticulospinal tract) results in the inhibition of the gamma discharge.

## Flaccid Paralysis of Muscles

Destruction of anterior horn cells, ventral nerve roots, or motor fibers of peripheral nerves abolishes both the voluntary and the reflex responses of muscles (Fig. 5). Besides paralysis, the affected muscles display no tonus and no tendon reflexes can be elicited. Within a few weeks the fibers of these muscles begin to show atrophy. They continue to shrink and, though some remnants may survive for several years, they ultimately disappear leaving only the interstitial connective tissue of the muscle. The atrophy of muscle fibers deprived of their motor neurons is more profound than the atrophy which occurs in muscles that are rendered inactive. Apparently the motor horn cell exerts a trophic influence on muscle fibers that is essential for maintaining their normal state. Muscles that are undergoing early stages of atrophy display fibrillary tremors and fasciculations. *Fibrillations* are fine twitchings of single muscle fibers, rarely visible except on the surface of exposed muscle. *Fasciculations* are brief contractions of a larger group of fibers which can be seen through the intact skin.

Lesions which damage fibers of the dorsal roots, or their cell bodies in spinal ganglia, also disrupt the stretch reflex path and, as a consequence, produce hypotonus and loss of tendon reflexes in muscles. In this instance the lower motor neurons remain intact and there is no loss of voluntary motor strength. The trophic influence of anterior horn cells is not impaired, and muscle atrophy or fasciculations do not appear.

## Spastic Paralysis of Muscles

A lesion that destroys the pyramidal tract prevents voluntary motor stimuli from reaching the anterior horn cells below the site of the injury and causes paralysis of the muscles supplied by these cells (Fig. 6). If the tract is interrupted suddenly, stretch reflexes are depressed temporarily, and the paralyzed muscles are flaccid. After an interval, which varies from a few days to a few weeks, stretch reflexes return in these muscles; furthermore, they usually become more active than normal. Increased tonus is demonstrated by firmness and stiffness, especially in the flexor muscles of the arm and the extensors of the leg. Muscle resistance to passive movements is exaggerated. This resistance is strong at the beginning of the movement but gives way in a peculiar clasp-knife fashion as more force is applied. Tendon reflexes are hyperactive. Occasionally a quick stretch of a tendon produces *clonus,* a sustained series of

13

rhythmic jerks, instead of a single contraction. Muscles that present these signs of hyperreflexia are said to be *spastic*, or to show *spasticity*. Other conditions may produce hypertonic muscles, but they have distinguishing features which differentiate them from the spasticity associated with lesions of the pyramidal tract. Some examples of these are decerebrate rigidity, reflex rigidity, catatonic rigidity, and myotonia.

The pyramidal tract, through its terminal fibers on lower motor neurons, was formerly thought to have the capacity of restricting the activity of the stretch reflex. Spasticity, consequently, was explained as the release of stretch reflexes from the inhibitory influence of the pyramidal tract. It is now believed that the activity of this reflex is regulated by the balanced effects of other fiber tracts which descend to the spinal cord from the brain stem. Some of these extrapyramidal fibers have suppressor effects, others are facilitatory. Since the suppressor fibers are located in close anatomical relation to the pyramidal tract, they are nearly always included in lesions that interrupt the pyramidal tract. The preponderant influence of the facilitatory fibers that remain undamaged is held responsible for spasticity. From a practical standpoint, spasticity remains a highly valued and reliable clinical sign of pyramidal tract damage, even though it may actually be caused by concurrent injury to accompanying extrapyramidal fibers.

The effects of lower motor neuron lesions are limited to the muscles that they innervate, but a small lesion that interrupts the pyramidal tract removes voluntary motor control from the whole sector of the body that lies down-stream from the level of injury. Thus destruction of the pyramidal tract in the upper cervical region of the spinal cord paralyzes the arm and the leg on the side of the lesion. If a similar lesion occurs at a site above the decussation of the tract, the paralysis will be in the arm and leg of the opposite side. Paralysis of this sort which includes both the arm and leg is termed *hemiplegia*. *Paraplegia* is paralysis of both legs as, for example, after a transverse lesion of the spinal cord that destroys both pyramidal tracts. Paralysis of a single extremity is *monoplegia*; one that includes all four extremities is *quadriplegia*. Lesions that impair function but are not severe enough to cause total paralysis produce weakness which is clinically designated as *paresis*.

## Other Reflexes Associated with Lesions of the Motor Pathway

Certain reflexes which are not elicited in normal individuals may be present after injuries of the pyramidal tract. *Babinski's sign* is an abnormal reflex obtained by stroking the plantar surface of the outer border of the foot with a blunt point. The normal response is plantar flexion of the toes, but if Babinski's sign is present, there is a slow dorsiflexion of the great toe accompanied by fanning of the lateral toes. When it is found, Babinski's sign is strong indication of a disorder of the pyramidal system. Many similar pathological reflexes have been described. *Hoffmann's sign* is sought by flicking the nail of the patient's middle finger. When it is present, there is prompt adduction of the thumb and flexion of the

14

index finger. Hoffman's sign is commonly associated with injury of the pyramidal tract, but it is also seen occasionally in normal persons.

Superficial reflexes which are normally obtained by stroking certain areas of the skin may be absent if the pyramidal tract is injured. If the skin of the abdominal wall is scratched gently, the umbilicus normally retracts in the direction of the stimulus. Stroking the upper, inner aspect of the thigh normally causes reflex contraction of the cremaster muscle with elevation of the testicle on the stimulated side. Loss of the *abdominal* or *cremasteric reflexes* confirms the presence of a pyramidal tract lesion, but absence of these reflexes bilaterally in an otherwise normal individual may have no significance.

destruction of pyramidal tract = cervical
region → paralys. of arm + leg on side
      of the lesion.

Lesion above decussation - paralys —
    arm + leg of the opposite side.

Paralysis of both arm + leg - hemiplegia
   "   of both legs   - paraplegia
   "   of a single extremity - monoplegia
   "   of all four extremit.  quadriplegia

Function impairmen but not paralysis
- called paresis.
Babinsky - disorder of pyramidal

15

## CHAPTER 4

# Proprioception; Stereognosis

## The Dorsal Roots and Dorsal Root Zones of the Spinal Cord

The dorsal roots of the spinal cord consist exclusively of sensory or afferent nerve fibers. All stimuli from the skin, and from internal structures as well, must pass through them to reach the spinal cord. The cell bodies of these fibers are located in spinal ganglia. Each ganglion cell possesses a single nerve process which divides like a "T," with a central branch running to the spinal cord and a peripheral branch coming from a receptor organ. There are no synapses in a spinal ganglion.

The area in which the dorsal root fibers enter the spinal cord, in the region of the dorsolateral sulcus, is called the *dorsal root zone*. The largest and most heavily myelinated fibers occupy the most medial position in this zone. Next to them are medium-sized fibers of tactile sense, and, on the lateral side of the root zone one finds thinly myelinated fine fibers of pain and temperature sense.

Many of the large calibered fibers are proprioceptive fibers coming chiefly from neuromuscular and neurotendinous spindles; a few come from Pacinian corpuscles between muscles and in joint capsules. The proprioceptive fibers conduct sensory reports from muscles, tendons, ligaments, and joints. These messages are essential for awareness of the position of the limbs and their movements, often referred to as the kinesthetic sense. The proprioceptive impulses which reach the central nervous system are not all directed to the sensory perception centers of the brain; some of them are distributed to other areas which do not function at a conscious level. The unconscious subdivision of the proprioceptive system is concerned with mechanisms of automatic motor control.

## Pathways of Proprioception in the Spinal Cord and Brain

After entering the spinal cord, proprioceptive fibers continue without synaptic interruption in three divergent routes (Fig. 7):

1. *Direct Fibers to Lower Motor Neurons in the Ventral Gray Horns.*

   These are the afferent fibers of the two neurons that make up the stretch reflex arc. They arise within a muscle spindle and end by synapse with motor cells within one or two spinal segments of the level at which they enter the spinal cord.

16

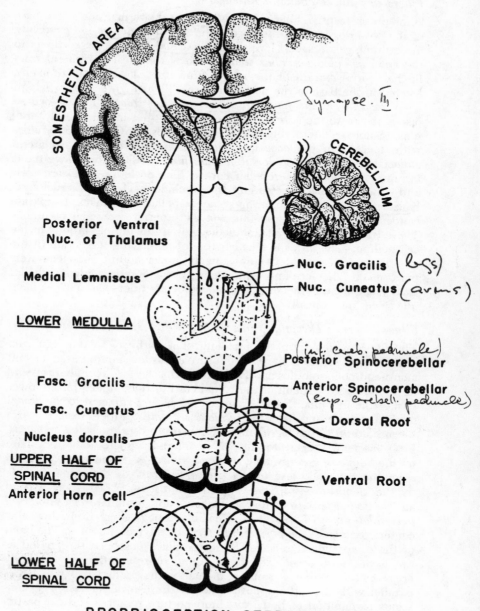

SOMESTHETIC AREA

Synapse. ᵢᵢᵢ

CEREBELLUM

Posterior Ventral
Nuc. of Thalamus

Medial Lemniscus

Nuc. Gracilis (legs)
Nuc. Cuneatus (arms)

LOWER MEDULLA

(inf. cereb. peduncle)
Posterior Spinocerebellar

Fasc. Gracilis

Fasc. Cuneatus

Nucleus dorsalis

Anterior Spinocerebellar
(sup. cerebell. peduncle)

Dorsal Root

UPPER HALF OF
SPINAL CORD
Anterior Horn Cell

Ventral Root

LOWER HALF OF
SPINAL CORD

PROPRIOCEPTION-STEREOGNOSIS

Lesion: loss of two point discriminat.
loss of limb position
Asteognosis
loss of vibratory
positive Rhomberg.

2. *Fibers to Spinocerebellar Pathways.*

Some proprioceptive fiber collaterals synapse with neurons in the base of the posterior horn of the cord. The *dorsal funicular gray nucleus,* in the lumbar and sacral levels, sends crossed and uncrossed fibers to the *anterior spinocerebellar* tract which is the most peripheral tract in the ventral margin of the lateral funiculus. The *nucleus dorsalis,* located in the base of the posterior horn (T1 to L1), sends ipsilateral fibers rostrally in the *posterior spinocerebellar tract* which is located just posterior to the anterior spinocerebellar tract in the lateral funiculus. Some collateral fibers from the levels of C1 to T5 synapse with neurons in the *accessory cuneate nucleus* to form ipsilateral *cuneocerebellar tract* or *dorsal arcuate fibers.* All of the above tracts terminate in the paleocerebellar cortex. The posterior spinocerebellar and cuneocerebellar tracts enter the cerebellum via the inferior cerebellar peduncle. The anterior spinocerebellar tract takes a separate course and enters the cerebellum via the superior cerebellar peduncle. These tracts report the instantaneous activity of muscle groups to the cerebellum. The latter is thus capable of modifying the action of the muscle groups so that the movements are smoothly and accurately performed. The forelimb equivalent of the anterior spinocerebellar tract (in the cat)—the rostral spinocerebellar tract—has not yet been identified anatomically.

3. *Fibers Turning Directly Upward in the Posterior Funiculus.*

The fibers which form the first link of a pathway to the cerebrum arise from receptors in the connective tissue (neuromuscular and neurotendinous spindles and Pacinian corpuscles). These fibers ascend in the posterior funiculi of the spinal cord to relay nuclei in the lower part of the medulla. Fibers from the leg ascend adjacent to the dorsal median septum and form the *fasciculus gracilis.* Fibers from the arm ascend lateral to the leg fibers and constitute the *fasciculus cuneatus.* Both fasciculi ascend to the lower medulla where they terminate in the *nucleus gracilis* and *nucleus cuneatus,* respectively. Fibers from the cells of these nuclei promptly cross to the opposite side in the *decussation of the medial lemniscus.* They then ascend as the *medial lemniscus* to the thalamus and terminate in the *ventral posterolateral (VPL) nucleus.* Thalamocortical fibers from this relay center continue to the *postcentral* gyrus of the parietal lobe. The band of the cortex which receives these terminals has been designated as the *somesthetic area.* The topographic representation of the body areas in this region is similar to that of the motor strip which lies parallel with it on the opposite side of the central sulcus. The conscious recognition of body and limb posture requires cortical participation.

In addition to fibers of proprioception, other fibers concerned with certain aspects of the sense of touch travel in the posterior funiculi, medial lemnisci, and thalamus to the postcentral gyri. This pathway to the cerebral cortex is necessary for *tactile discrimination*: the ability to appreciate two separate points at which pressure is applied simultane-

18

ously; to recognize the size, shape and texture of objects by feeling; and to identify letters and figures drawn on the skin by touch. Such faculty is known as *stereognosis*, the ability to recognize form; its absence is designated as *astereognosis*.

## Disturbances of Sensation Following Interruption of the Proprioceptive Pathway of the Brain

Lesions which damage the conscious proprioceptive pathway produce defects in muscle sense and in stereognosis. The symptoms seem to be more prominent after injury of the posterior funiculi, but they are also found, in varying degree, with lesions of the gracile and cuneate nuclei, the medial lemniscus, thalamus, or postcentral gyrus. A patient with bilateral posterior funiculus damage suffers ataxia (loss of muscular coordination) which causes a marked disturbance of gait. Unless he can watch the movements of the limbs and voluntarily correct errors, he stumbles, staggers and may fall.

*Clinical signs* of injury to the funiculus frequently tested in a neurological examination are:

1. *Inability to Recognize Limb Position.*

   The patient is unable to say, without looking, whether a joint is put in a position of flexion or extension.

2. *Asterognosis.*

   There is loss, or impairment, of the ability to recognize common objects, such as keys, coins, blocks, marbles, etc., by touching and handling them with the eyes closed.

3. *Loss of Two Point Discrimination.*

   There is loss of the normal facility of recognizing two points simultaneously applied to the skin as distinct from one single point. The two points of a compass may be used for testing.

4. *Loss of Vibratory Sense.*

   A vibrating tuning fork applied by the base to a bony prominence is normally perceived as a "buzzy," mildly tingling sensation. When this ability is lost, the patient cannot differentiate between a vibrating fork and a silent one.

5. *Positive Romberg Sign.*

   In this test the patient is asked to stand with the feet placed close together. The amount of body sway is noted while the eyes are open, then compared with the degree of sway present with the eyes closed. An abnormal accentuation of sway, or an actual loss of balance, with the eyes closed is a *positive* result. Visual sense is able to compensate, in part, for a deficiency in conscious recognition of muscle and joint posture. Therefore the patient may be able to maintain his balance if he is allowed to open his eyes. Symptoms of ataxia caused by lesions of the cerebellum are, on the contrary, not corrected by visual compensation.

# CHAPTER 5

# Pain and Temperature Senses

## The Pain-Temperature Pathway

The peripheral receptors for pain sense are naked terminals of branching networks of fine nerve fibers. Pain fibers enter the spinal cord in the lateral part of the dorsal root zone and divide at once into short ascending and descending branches which run longitudinally in the *dorsolateral fasciculus*. Within a segment or two they leave this tract to synapse with neurons in the *substantia gelatinosa (of Rolando)*. Axons of the latter neurons cross to the opposite side ventral to the central canal within one or two spinal segments of the level at which the dorsal root fibers enter. After crossing, the fibers turn upward in the *lateral spinothalamic tract* which is located in the ventral one-half of the lateral funiculus. The tract extends without interruption through the spinal cord, medulla, pons and midbrain to the ventral posterolateral nucleus of the thalamus. Thalamocortical fibers from this sensory relay nucleus establish the final connection to the postcentral gyrus of the parietal lobe (Fig. 8).

Pain fibers from the face, the cornea of the eye, and the mucosa of the lips, cheeks and tongue are carried in the trigeminal nerve and its sensory ganglion (the semilunar ganglion). Upon entering the brain stem in the pontile region these fibers form a descending tract—the *descending, or spinal root of the trigeminal nerve.* Terminals of the spinal root of the trigeminal nerve make synapses in an adjacent nucleus which is similar in appearance to the substantia gelatinosa of the spinal cord. Axons of the nucleus of the spinal root of the trigeminal nerve cross to the opposite side and ascend to the ventral posteromedial nucleus of the thalamus which relays pain impulses to the postcentral gyrus of the parietal lobe.

## Perception of Pain

Painful stimuli are recognized consciously when nerve impulses arrive at the thalamus by way of the pain pathway. Other qualities besides the crude perception of pain as such are not appreciated by the thalamus but are supplied by the parietal cortex, where pain stimuli are integrated with other sensory stimuli. Pain is associated with an unpleasant subjective feeling and is capable of arousing strong emotional protest. The disagreeable aspect of pain can be accentuated or depressed by mental and emotional states without any real change in the physiologic threshold for pain.

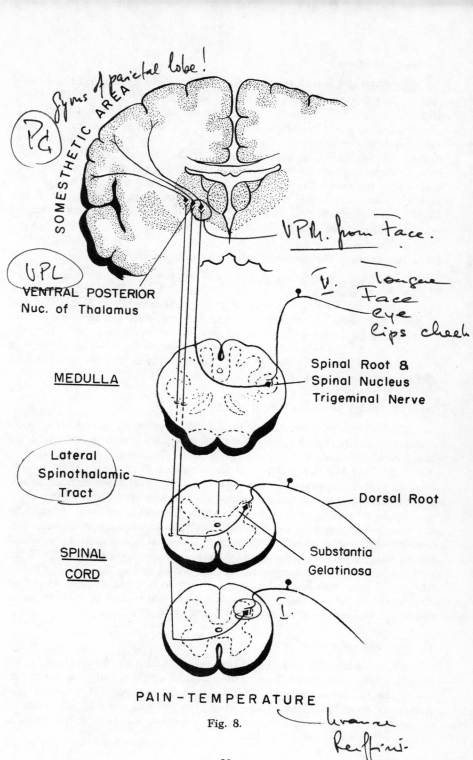

Gyrus of parietal lobe!

Pc

SOMESTHETIC AREA

VPM from Face.

UPL
VENTRAL POSTERIOR
Nuc. of Thalamus

V. Tongue
Face
eye
lips cheek

MEDULLA

Spinal Root &
Spinal Nucleus
Trigeminal Nerve

Lateral
Spinothalamic
Tract

Dorsal Root

SPINAL
CORD

Substantia
Gelatinosa

I.

PAIN - TEMPERATURE

Fig. 8.

Lorenze
Renftini

21

## Temperature Sense

The receptors in the skin for the sense of cold are thought to be the end bulbs of Krause; for warmth, the end bulbs of Ruffini. The fibers and cells serving the sensory path for temperature perception follow the same course as those of the pain pathway. The two systems are so closely associated in the central nervous system that they can scarcely be distinguished anatomically, and an injury to one usually affects the other to a similar degree. Testing either pain or temperature sensibility accomplishes the same result. If pain sense is normal, pricking the skin with a sharp point is reported as feeling "sharp" rather than "dull." Or tubes filled with warm and cool water may be applied to the skin to determine whether differences in temperature can be felt.

## Effect of Cutting the Lateral Spinothalamic Tract

The lateral spinothalamic tracts are sometimes sectioned in humans to relieve intractable pain—a surgical procedure known as *tractotomy.* The cut is made in the ventral part of the lateral funiculus. Some damage is done to the anterior spinocerebellar tract, and perhaps to certain extrapyramidal motor fibers, but no permanent symptoms are produced except loss of pain sensibility on the contralateral side, beginning one or two segments below the cut. Bilateral tractotomy is usually necessary to abolish pain from visceral organs.

## Sensory Effects of Dorsal Root Irritation

Mechanical compression, or local inflammation, of dorsal nerve roots irritates pain fibers and commonly produces pain which is felt along the anatomical distribution of the roots affected. The area of skin supplied by one dorsal root is a *dermatome,* or skin segment. The approximate boundaries of human dermatomes are shown in Fig. 9. Pain which is limited in distribution to one or more dermatomes is known as *radicular pain.*

Sensory changes other than pain may be associated with dorsal root irritation. There may be localized areas of *paresthesia*—spontaneous sensations of prickling, tingling, or numbness. Zones of *hyperesthesia*, in which tactile stimuli appear to be grossly exaggerated, may be present. If the pathological process is a progressive one which gradually destroys fibers, the dorsal roots will finally lose their ability to conduct sensory impulses. There will be *hypesthesia* (diminished sensitivity) and eventually *anesthesia* (the complete absence of all forms of sensibility).

## Visceral Pain—Referred Pain

The parenchyma of internal organs, including the brain itself, is not supplied with pain receptors. The walls of arteries, all peritoneal surfaces, pleural membranes and the dura mater covering the brain may be sources of severe pain, especially when they are subjected to inflammation or mechanical traction. Abnormal contraction or dilation of the walls of hollow viscera also causes pain.

Pain of visceral origin is apt to be vaguely localized. At times it is felt in a surface area of the body far removed from its actual source, a phenomenon known as *referred pain*. For example: the pain of coronary heart disease may be felt in the chest wall, left axilla or down the inside of the left arm; inflammation of the peritoneum covering the diaphragm

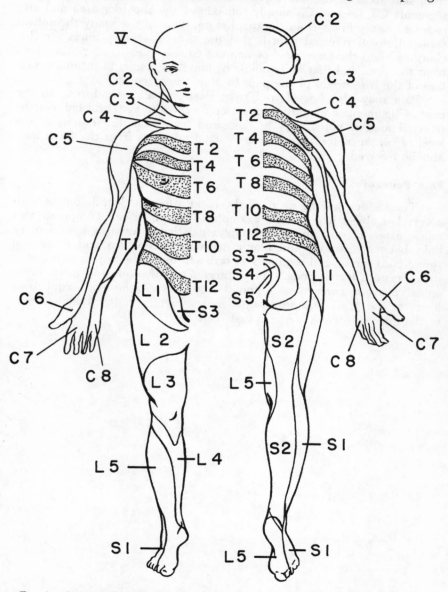

Fig. 9.   Segmental areas of innervation of the skin. Overlapping of one segment occurs between adjacent dermatomes.

may be felt over the shoulder. In each case the neurons that supply the skin area in which the pain is felt enter the same segment of the spinal cord as do the neurons which actually conduct the pain stimuli from the visceral organ. Spinal cord segments T1 and T2 receive sensory fibers from skin areas of the left upper extremity and from the heart as well; segments C3, C4 and C5 supply the skin of the shoulder area and also receive sensory fibers from the diaphragm. One of the many theoretical explanations of referred pain is that the visceral sensory fibers are discharging into the same pool of neurons in the spinal cord as the fibers from the skin, and that an overflow of impulses results in misinterpretation of the true origin of the pain by the sensory cortex.

Pain may also be referred from deep somatic structures. In the case of ligaments and muscles associated with the vertebral column the referred area is not always in the same segmental distribution as the level of origin of the pain impulses. Pain impulses from the teeth may also be referred.

### Pain Reflexes

The sudden jerking away of the hand after accidental contact with a very hot object is a familiar example of a pain reflex. To operate this reflex, axons of cells of the substantia gelatinosa serve as intermediary links between sensory and motor neurons, passing up and down the spinal cord for several segments in order to make the appropriate lower motor neuron connections. These internuncial neurons and other intraspinal neurons connecting different segments of the cord contribute fibers to the *fasciculus proprius*, a zone of white matter that lies next to the gray substance of the spinal cord.

## CHAPTER 6

# Touch Sense

Under ordinary circumstances tactile sensations are complex in nature since they involve the blending of a number of more elementary components. Two different forms of touch sensibility are recognized: (1) *Simple touch* is concerned with the sense of light touch, light pressure, and a crude sense of tactile localization. Tickling sensation should also be included in this category, but itching is more clearly related to pain sense. (2) *Tactile discrimination* conveys the sense of deeper pressure, spatial localization, and the perception of the size and shape of objects.

## The Pathway of Simple Touch

The peripheral receptors are tactile corpuscles in the dermis of the skin and networks of nerve terminals around hair follicles. The myelinated fibers which convey sensory impulses from these endings enter the spinal cord by way of dorsal roots. These fibers eventually make synapses with certain cells of the central part of the posterior gray horns, the *nucleus proprius* or central magnocellular column, but they do not do so until a considerable amount of longitudinal dispersion has taken place. Some branches of the entering root fibers reach the nucleus proprius of the posterior gray matter within one or two segments. Other branches may extend 10 to 15 segments upward in the posterior funiculi before synapsing in the gray matter of the spinal cord. The second fibers of the pathway arise from cells of the posterior gray horn, cross in the anterior white commissure and turn upward in the *anterior spinothalamic tract* of the opposite side (Fig. 10). The anterior spinothalamic tract, smaller and somewhat more diffuse than the lateral spinothalamic tract, is located near the periphery of the anterior funiculus. It takes a direct, upward course through the spinal cord and brain stem and ends in the ventral posterolateral nucleus of the thalamus. After synapsing here, thalamocortical fibers relay sensory impulses to the postcentral gyrus of the cerebrum.

## Effect of Cutting the Anterior Spinothalamic Tract

Of all types of skin sensibility, simple touch is least likely to be impaired by lesions of the spinal cord. It is not abolished by destruction of the anterior spinothalamic tract on one side, possibly because such a

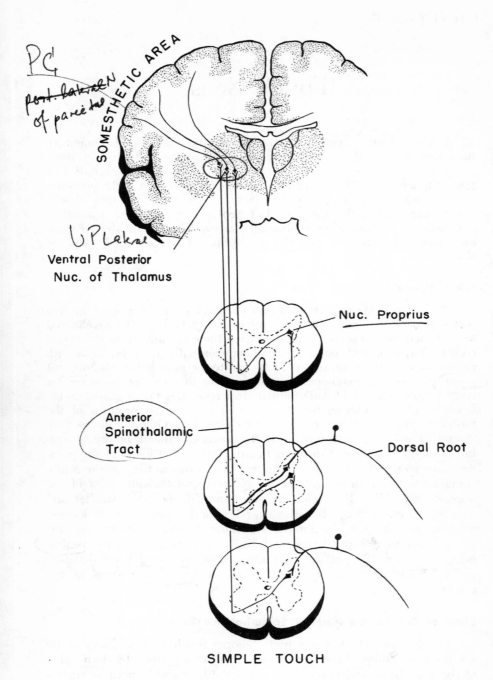

PC'
post. lateral N
of parietal

SOMESTHETIC AREA

U P Lateral

Ventral Posterior
Nuc. of Thalamus

Nuc. Proprius

Anterior
Spinothalamic
Tract

Dorsal Root

SIMPLE TOUCH

Fig. 10.

lesion fails to block sensory impulses in the collateral branches of entering root fibers. Many of these uncrossed, ascending branches pass high enough to maintain a path which joins the anterior spinothalamic tract above the level of an injury (Fig. 11). Impulses are thus able to bypass a defect in the tract and no appreciable loss of simple touch sense is noticed. If the lesion is located in the cervical region of the spinal cord, most of the simple touch fibers from the lower extremity will be disconnected. Then, some loss of light touch sense in the leg on the opposite side may be demonstrable. To explain the persistence of some light touch sensibility after a cervical cord lesion it has been postulated that this function may be partly duplicated by touch fibers in the fasciculi gracilis and cuneatus.

The routine method of testing *simple touch* is by stroking the skin with a wisp of cotton. This is sufficient for ordinary purposes, but it does not bring out partial loss of sensibility. Von Frey hairs are used for experimental work. These are a series of fine hairs of graduated stiffness for applying stimuli of calibrated intensity to the skin.

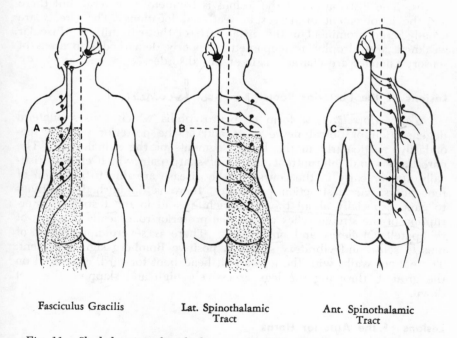

Fasciculus Gracilis        Lat. Spinothalamic        Ant. Spinothalamic
                        Tract                  Tract

Fig. 11.   Shaded regions show body areas affected by interrupting sensory paths at the mid-thoracic level of the spinal cord:
      A.   Section of the posterior funiculus (left).
      B.   Section of the lateral spinothalamic tract (left).
      C.   Section of the anterior spinothalamic tract (left).

## CHAPTER 7

# Lesions of Nerves and Spinal Cord

## Lesions of Peripheral Nerves

Injury of an individual peripheral nerve is followed by paralysis of muscles and loss of sensation limited to those muscles and skin areas supplied by the nerve distal to the lesion. The paralyzed muscles are flaccid and gradually undergo severe atrophy. All forms of sensation including proprioception are lost. Recognition of peripheral nerve lesions is based on knowledge of the gross anatomy of the course and distribution of such nerves.

In *multiple neuritis* there is partial destruction of various peripheral nerves. The distribution of the lesions is frequently bilateral, but there may be involvement of nerves in scattered locations. The effects are usually more prominent in the distal parts of the extremities. Muscular weakness and atrophy accompanied by poorly demarked skin areas of sensory changes are characteristic of this disorder.

## Lesions of the Posterior Roots *positive Romberg.*

*Tabes dorsalis* is a form of neurosyphilis which causes bilateral degeneration of dorsal nerve roots and of the posterior funiculi secondarily, particularly in the lower segments of the spinal cord. The paresthesias and intermittent attacks of sharp pain which characteristically appear early in the course of the disease are due to irritation of root fibers. As destruction progresses, there is diminished sensitivity to pain, especially about the tendo achillis and in the testicles. Interruption of the stretch reflex arcs in the posterior roots leads to a loss of the patellar reflexes and ankle jerks. There is severe impairment of muscle sense and vibratory sense. A positive Romberg sign is present. The patient walks with the legs apart, head bent forward, eyes fixed on the ground, throwing the legs excessively high and slapping the feet down.

## Lesions of the Anterior Horns

*Acute poliomyelitis,* or infantile paralysis, is caused by a virus which selects anterior horn cells, particularly in the cervical and lumbar enlargements of the spinal cord, often damaging them in large numbers. The extent of the muscle paralysis and the muscle groups affected varies, depending on the distribution of motor cells which fail to recover. Paralyzed muscles are flaccid and their reflexes are usually absent.

Atrophy develops after several weeks, and paralyzed muscles may ultimately be entirely replaced by connective and adipose tissue. Severe paralysis is likely to result in extensive deformities.

## Lesions of the Central Gray Matter *lat. spinothal. (loss of pain) + temp.*

In *syringomyelia* there is softening and cavitation around the central canal of the spinal cord, most commonly in the region of the cervical enlargement. A lesion in this position interrupts the lateral spinothalamic fibers which pass ventral to the central canal as they cross from one side to the other. Since these fibers conduct pain and temperature impulses from dermatomes on both sides of the body, the result is loss of pain and temperature sensibility with segmental distribution in the upper extremities on both sides. The spinothalamic tracts themselves remain intact, so there is no sensory impairment in the lower extremities. Proprioception and the sense of simple touch are spared in the affected dermatomes of the arms. A condition such as this in which one type of skin sense is lost and others preserved is referred to as *sensory dissociation.* In later stages of the disease, degeneration often extends to the anterior gray horns and causes paralysis with atrophy of muscles innervated by the segments which are involved. Signs of pyramidal tract damage may appear in the lower extremities as a result of compression by the cystic cavity.

## Lesions Involving Both the Anterior Horns and the Pyramidal Tracts

*Amyotrophic lateral sclerosis* is a fatal disease (cause unknown) characterized by destruction of motor cells in the anterior gray horns of the spinal cord together with degeneration of the pyramidal tracts bilaterally. Sensory changes are usually not found. There is weakness and atrophy of some muscles, with spasticity and hyperreflexia in others. The effects may be somewhat irregular in distribution, depending on individual variations in the pattern of the lesions in the spinal cord. The classical form of this disease starts with weakness, atrophy and fasciculations of the muscles of the hands and arms, followed later by spastic paralysis of the legs. Motor nuclei of cranial nerves in some cases undergo degeneration.

## Lesions Involving Both the Posterior and the Lateral Funiculi *loss of position sense + vibration.*

*Subacute combined degeneration* is a disease of the spinal cord most often seen in pernicious anemia but sometimes occurring with other anemias or nutritional disturbances. The posterior funiculi and the pyramidal tracts of the spinal cord undergo degeneration, but the gray matter is ordinarily not affected. Injury of the posterior funiculi is accompanied by loss of position sense in the lower extremities, impairment of ability to recognize vibration over the legs and a positive Romberg sign. Motor weakness in the legs, with spasticity, hyperactive tendon reflexes and bilateral Babinski signs, indicate degeneration of the pyramidal tracts.

29

## Thrombosis of the Anterior Spinal Artery

The anterior spinal artery runs in the anterior median sulcus and sends terminal branches to supply the ventral and lateral portions of the spinal cord. The anterior horns, the lateral spinothalamic tracts and the pyramidal tracts are included in its territory, but the posterior funiculi and posterior horns are supplied independently by a pair of posterior spinal arteries. Thrombosis of the anterior spinal artery in the cervical region of the cord produces atrophy, fibrillation and flaccid paralysis at the level of the lesion due to destruction of anterior horn cells. There will also be spastic paraplegia from pyramidal tract involvement and, usually, loss of pain and temperature sense below the lesion due to lateral spinothalamic damage. The onset of symptoms is abrupt and is often accompanied by severe pain.

*post. spinal Aa : post. funiculi + post. horn.*

## Hemisection of the Spinal Cord

Lateral hemisection of the spinal cord (as, for example, from a bullet or knife wound) produces the *Brown-Séquard syndrome*. The specific effects and the injured structures that account for them are summarized as follows:

*From Injury to Fiber Tracts*

I. On the side of the lesion:

*same side*

  a. *Pyramidal tract* damage: motor paralysis below the injury with spasticity, hyperactivity reflexes, loss of superficial reflexes and Babinski's sign.

  b. *Posterior funiculus* damage: loss of muscle and position sense; loss of vibratory sense and tactile discrimination below the injury. (Because of the paralysis, ataxia which might otherwise occur cannot be readily demonstrated.)

II. On the side opposite the lesion:

*opposite side.*

  a. *Lateral spinothalamic tract* damage: loss of sensation of pain and temperature beginning one or two dermatomes below the injury.

  b. *Anterior spinothalamic tract* damage: little or no objective change in the sense of simple touch.

*From Injury to Local Cord Segments and Nerve Roots*

Besides the effects produced by interrupting the long ascending and descending tracts of the spinal cord, there are likely to be additional symptoms from damage to dorsal and ventral nerve roots at the level of the injury. When these are present, they are of great value in localizing the individual cord segments involved.

I. On the side of the lesion:

  a. Irritation of fibers in the *dorsal root zone*: paresthesias, or radicular pain in a band over the affected dermatomes.

b. Destruction of *dorsal roots*: a band of anesthesia over the dermatome supplied by the involved roots.

c. Destruction of *ventral roots*: flaccid paralysis affecting only those muscles innervated by fibers which have been destroyed.

Few lesions are precisely localized to one lateral half of the spinal cord. More often they involve one sector of the cord and produce a partial, or incomplete Brown-Séquard syndrome. The particular symptoms and signs of each individual case are determined by the position and extent of the lesion.

## Tumors of the Spinal Cord

Tumors that arise outside the spinal cord (extramedullary tumors) gradually impinge on the cord as they enlarge. Compression of nerve roots is likely to occur first and is responsible for pain distributed over the dermatomes supplied by these roots. This is followed by gradual involvement of the tracts within the cord until a Brown-Séquard syndrome, or some modification of it, is reached. The order of appearance of symptoms may furnish a clue to the site of the tumor. For example, loss of pain and temperature on the left side followed by spastic paralysis on the right implies that the tumor has arisen from the ventrolateral region of the cord on the right side. Loss of proprioception sense on the right side followed by an extension of proprioceptive deficit to the left side and

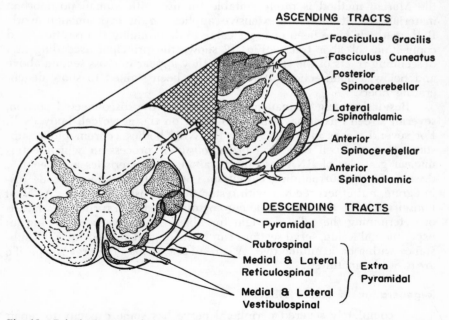

**ASCENDING TRACTS**

Fasciculus Gracilis
Fasciculus Cuneatus
Posterior Spinocerebellar
Lateral Spinothalamic
Anterior Spinocerebellar
Anterior Spinothalamic

**DESCENDING TRACTS**

Pyramidal
Rubrospinal
Medial & Lateral Reticulospinal
Medial & Lateral Vestibulospinal

Extra Pyramidal

Fig. 12. Principal tracts of the spinal cord. The descending tracts are shown in the lower cross section; ascending tracts in the upper section. Shaded areas correspond to the regions of degeneration above and below a hemisection of the cord.

31

the development of spastic paralysis on the right, indicates that the tumor is compressing the cord from the dorsomedial region on the right side.

Injuries to nerve fibers vary in degree. Some are sufficient to prevent conduction of nerve impulses without causing irreversible fiber degeneration. The pressure of tumors, intervertebral discs, blood clots, or the swelling and edema of wounds may produce cord symptoms that are later alleviated by treatment. The prospect of recovery depends on the pressure and its duration.

## Degenerative Changes in Nerve Cells

When a fiber is transected or permanently destroyed, the part which has been separated from the nerve cell body degenerates completely and, in the process, loses its myelin sheath. Degenerated fibers can be studied histologically by obtaining a series of microscopic sections, staining them appropriately and reconstructing the course of the fibers. The *Weigert method* employs a modified hematoxylin stain which stains normal myelin dark blue or black. An unstained area appearing in the position normally occupied by a fiber tract indicates degeneration. The *Marchi method* utilizes impregnation of the sections with osmium tetroxide to blacken degenerating nerve fibers while leaving normal myelinated fibers unstained. It is only effective if it is applied at a particular stage of the degenerative process when myelin is partly, but not completely, chemically decomposed (generally 6 to 12 days after injury). For this reason the Marchi method is rarely suitable for use with human postmortem material, but it finds an extensive application in experimental work. Both methods have been of great value in determining the positions and connections of fiber tracts. Fig. 12 shows the principal ascending and descending tracts of the spinal cord as they appear in cross section above and below a hemisection after they have been stained to show degenerating fibers.

Besides causing permanent destruction of the disconnected portion, severing a cell's axon has a harmful effect on the nerve cell body itself. For several weeks after the injury the Nissl bodies (chromophilic substance) of the cell undergo *chromatolysis*—a process in which extranuclear granules of RNA lose their staining characteristics and seem to dissolve in the surrounding cytoplasm. Some of the affected cells disintegrate, but others recover with restoration of Nissl substance. As Nissl himself realized, this retrograde chromatolytic reaction furnishes a means of determining the cells of origin for fibers. Some weeks following an experimental lesion, serial sections can be made and stained for Nissl substance with a basic aniline dye. A careful search may then reveal specific areas of chromatolysis.

## Regeneration of Nerve Fibers

A completely severed peripheral nerve has some capacity to repair itself. *Neurilemma cells* from the isolated stump proliferate and attempt to bridge the gap with the distal end of the nerve. The axis cylinders in the cut, central end of the nerve divide longitudinally and soon begin to sprout out of the end of the nerve. Many sprouting axons go astray in random directions, but some of them cross the gap and enter neurilemmal tubes leading to the peripheral endings. Their rate of growth is normally 1 to 2 mm. per day. Chance apparently determines whether a regenerating motor fiber enters a neurilemmal tube leading to a motor or to a sensory terminal. If suitably matched, connections with a motor end-plate can be re-established and function restored.

Fibers of the brain and of the spinal cord do not regenerate effectively.

## CHAPTER 8

# Brain Stem

The brain stem is divided into the following portions: medulla, pons, midbrain and diencephalon.

## MEDULLA

The medulla (medulla oblongata) (bulb) is continuous with the spinal cord at the foramen magnum and extends some 2.5 cm. to the caudal border of the pons. The central canal of the spinal cord continues through the caudal half of the medulla, and then, at a point called the *obex,* flares open into the wide cavity of the *fourth ventricle* dorsally. The dorsal surface of the upper half of the medulla thus occupies the lateral floor of the ventricle. The roof of this part of the medulla is formed by the *chorioid plexus,* a thin sheet of ependyma and pia mater.

### External Markings of the Medulla

*Ventral Aspect* (Fig. 13). The *pyramids,* which contain the pyramidal tracts, form two longitudinal ridges on either side of the anterior median fissure. Their decussation can be seen obliterating the fissure at the extreme caudal end of the medulla.

*Lateral Aspect* (Fig. 14). Two longitudinal grooves are present. The *ventrolateral sulcus* extends along the lateral border of the pyramid and contains the row of rootlets of the hypoglossal nerve (n. XII). Radicles of the accessory nerve (n. XI), vagus nerve (n. X), and glossopharyngeal nerve (n. IX) are attached in line along the *dorsolateral sulcus.* The prominent oval swelling of the lateral area between these sulci is the *olive.* This marks the site of the inferior olivary nucleus inside the medulla.

*Dorsal Aspect* (Fig. 15). The fasciculus gracilis and the fasciculus cuneatus are visible as low ridges. The sites of the nucleus gracilis and the nucleus cuneatus are marked by small eminences named, respectively, the *clava* and the *cuneate tubercle.* Rostral to the obex, separation of the left and right dorsal plates of the medulla exposes the floor of the fourth ventricle. The two prominent ridges extending along the sides of the ventricle are the *inferior cerebellar peduncles* (restiform bodies). Two pairs of small swellings can be seen in the floor of the ventricle. Their tapering margins point caudally and gradually meet the groove of the medial sulcus in a configuration named the *calamus scriptorius* from its resemblance to the point of a pen. The lateral ridges of the calamus constitute the *vagal trigone;* the medial ridges are the *hypoglossal trigone.* Rostral to the *stria of the fourth* ventricle is the *facial colliculus.* The

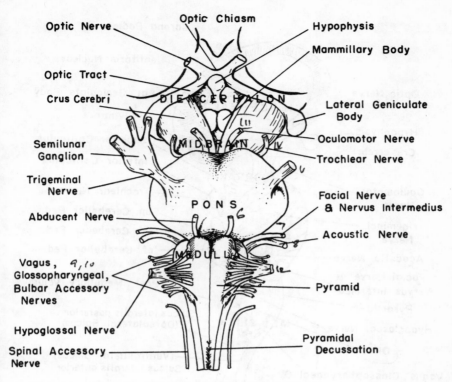

Fig. 13.　Ventral view of the brain stem.

rostral continuation of the ridge is known as the *median eminence*. The groove on the lateral margin of these central ridges is the *sulcus limitans* which demarcates the sensory and motor areas of the medulla.

### Internal Structures of the Medulla

Some of the long fiber tracts of the spinal cord pass directly through the medulla without any major changes in their relative positions, but otherwise the arrangement of fibers and gray substance of the medulla is more complex than in the spinal cord.

*Lower Half of the Medulla* (Figs. 16 and 17). The *central canal* is surrounded by a *central gray area* which is modified at its perimeter to become a diffuse zone containing a network of fibers and scattered cells known as the *reticular formation*. The reticular formation extends through the medulla, pons and mesencephalon. The *pyramidal tracts* occupy the most ventral part of the medulla and, at this point, are crossing in a prominent *decussation* which brings them to the lateral position that they maintain in the spinal cord. On the dorsal side the *fasciculi gracilis* and *cuneatus* are still present, but the nuclei in which their fibers terminate have appeared. Axons of the cells in these nuclei take a downward, arched course forming the *internal arcuate fibers* which cross the midline

35

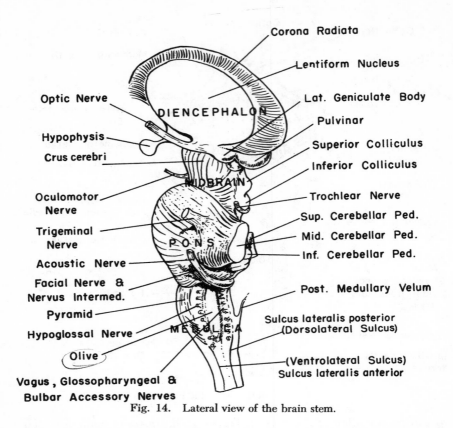

Corona Radiata
Lentiform Nucleus
Optic Nerve
DIENCEPHALON
Lat. Geniculate Body
Pulvinar
Hypophysis
Crus cerebri
Superior Colliculus
Inferior Colliculus
MIDBRAIN
Oculomotor Nerve
Trochlear Nerve
Sup. Cerebellar Ped.
Trigeminal Nerve
PONS
Mid. Cerebellar Ped.
Inf. Cerebellar Ped.
Acoustic Nerve
Facial Nerve & Nervus Intermed.
Post. Medullary Velum
Pyramid
Hypoglossal Nerve
MEDULLA
Sulcus lateralis posterior (Dorsolateral Sulcus)
Olive
(Ventrolateral Sulcus)
Sulcus lateralis anterior
Vagus, Glossopharyngeal & Bulbar Accessory Nerves

Fig. 14.   Lateral view of the brain stem.

as the *decussation of the medial lemniscus.* In the dorsolateral region a clear nuclear area, capped by a peripheral zone of fine fibers, represents the *spinal tract* and *spinal nucleus* of the *trigeminal nerve.* The latter structures remain in the same relative position as they descend from the pontile region.

*Upper Half of the Medulla* (Fig. 18). The *inferior olivary nucleus* is a prominent structure in the ventrolateral region resembling a crinkled sac with an opening directed toward the midline. Many of its efferent fibers cross and stream toward the dorsolateral corner of the medulla to join spinocerebellar fibers in the thick, *inferior cerebellar peduncle.* Other olivocerebellar fibers enter the peduncle without crossing.

Three distinct cellular areas (symmetrically paired) occupy the dorsal part of the medulla close to the floor of the ventricle. Since they extend longitudinally through the upper medulla, they represent three nuclear columns. The *nucleus of the hypoglossal nerve* (n. XII) is nearest the midline. Fibers of this nerve pass ventrally to emerge between the pyramid and the olive. The *dorsal motor nucleus* of the vagus nerve (n. X) lies at the side of the hypoglossal nucleus. The most lateral nuclear column, demarcated by the sulcus limitans, contains the *vestibular group of nuclei* which receives afferent fibers from the vestibular division of the acoustic nerve (n. VIII).

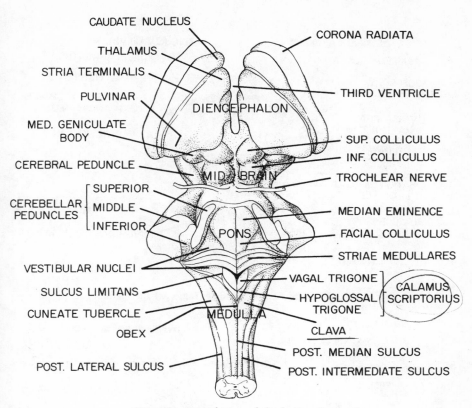

Fig. 15. Dorsal view of the brain stem.

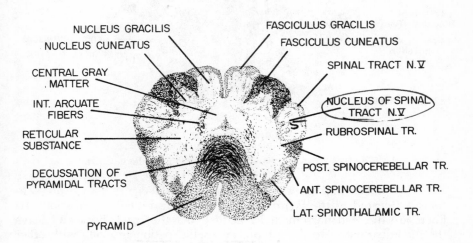

Fig. 16. Cross section of the extreme lower region of the medulla.

37

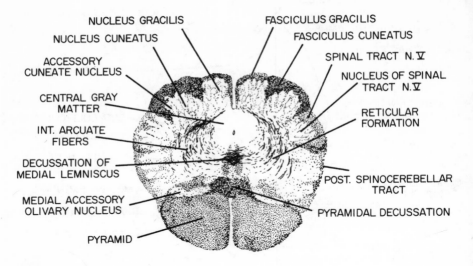

Fig. 17. Cross section of the lower region of the medulla.

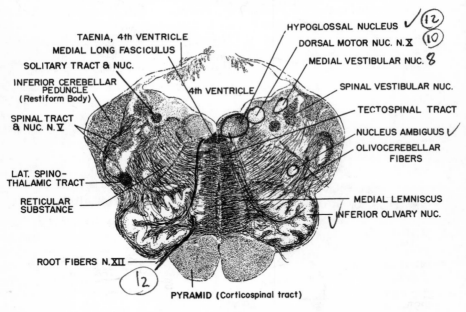

Fig. 18. Cross section of the upper region of the medulla.

The *nucleus ambiguus*, seen indistinctly in Weigert stained preparations, is located in the ventrolateral part of the reticular formation. Its fibers are directed dorsomedially at first, but they arch back and leave the medulla ventral to the inferior cerebellar peduncle along with other fibers of the vagus nerve. An isolated bundle of longitudinal fibers accompanied by a small nucleus appears in the dorsal part of the reticular

38

formation. It is known as the *solitary tract* and is made up of afferent root fibers of the vagal system. The nucleus which lies beside it is the *nucleus of the solitary tract.*

The lateral spinothalamic tract is adjacent to the nucleus ambiguus on its ventrolateral side. Two large bands of fibers lie vertically at either side of the midline. The extreme dorsal portions of these bands contain the *medial longitudinal fasciculus, tectospinal* and *medial vestibulospinal tracts;* the remainder comprise the *medial lemnisci.*


## PONS

The pons (pons varolii) is a large oblong-shaped mass rostral to the medulla. The cerebral peduncles pass into it from above, and the pyramids emerge from its caudal margin.

### External Markings of the Pons

*Ventral Aspect* (Fig. 13). The surface is entirely occupied by a band of thick transverse fibers which constitutes the pons proper. A shallow furrow (the basal sulcus) extends along the midline coinciding with the course of the basilar artery. The abducent nerves (n. VI) take exit in the inferior pontine sulcus at the caudal border of the pons close to the pyramids.

*Lateral Aspect* (Fig. 14). The transverse fibers of the pons are funnelled into compact lateral bundles—the *middle cerebellar peduncles* (brachia pontis)—which attach the pons to the overlying cerebellum. The triangular space formed between the caudal border of the middle cerebellar peduncle, the adjoining part of the cerebellum, and the upper part of the medulla is the *pontocerebellar angle.* The *facial nerve* (n. VII) and the *acoustic nerve* (n. VIII) are attached to the brain stem in this niche. The *trigeminal nerve* (n. V)—one of the largest of the cranial nerves—penetrates the brachium pontis near the middle of the lateral surface of the pons.

*Dorsal Aspect* (Fig. 15). The dorsal surface of the pons forms the rostral floor of the fourth ventricle. It is a triangular area with its widest point at the pontomedullary junction where the lateral recesses of the ventricle are situated. Faint transverse striations observed in this region are named the *striae medullares* which are really formed by arcuocerebellar fibers totally unrelated to the acoustic system. The two bands which course along the sides of the triangular space are the *superior cerebellar peduncles* (brachia conjunctiva). The anterior *medullary velum* is a thin layer of tissue completing the roof of the ventricle.

### Internal Structure of the Pons

Two subdivisions are evident—a dorsal portion known as the *tegmentum,* and a ventral part called the *basilar portion of the pons.* In this region of the brain stem the roof portion, overlying the cavity of the ventricle, has become expanded and specialized to form the cerebellum.

*Caudal Portion* (Fig. 19). The pyramidal tracts are located centrally in the basilar portion. The gray matter which surrounds them contains the cells of the *pontile nuclei*. Transverse fibers crossing from one side to the other dorsal and ventral to the pyramidal tracts are the axons of the pontile nuclei. They enter the *middle cerebellar peduncle* and pass to the cortex of the cerebellum.

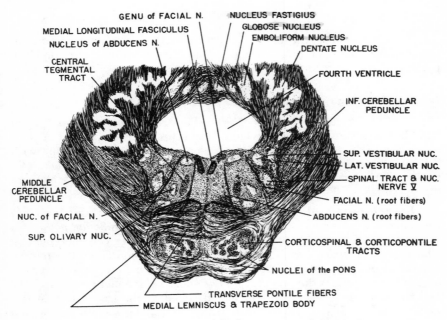

GENU of FACIAL N.
NUCLEUS FASTIGIUS
MEDIAL LONGITUDINAL FASCICULUS
GLOBOSE NUCLEUS
NUCLEUS of ABDUCENS N.
EMBOLIFORM NUCLEUS
DENTATE NUCLEUS
CENTRAL TEGMENTAL TRACT
FOURTH VENTRICLE
INF. CEREBELLAR PEDUNCLE
SUP. VESTIBULAR NUC.
LAT. VESTIBULAR NUC.
SPINAL TRACT & NUC. NERVE Ⅴ
MIDDLE CEREBELLAR PEDUNCLE
FACIAL N. ( root fibers )
NUC. of FACIAL N.
ABDUCENS N. ( root fibers )
SUP. OLIVARY NUC.
CORTICOSPINAL & CORTICOPONTILE TRACTS
NUCLEI of the PONS
TRANSVERSE PONTILE FIBERS
MEDIAL LEMNISCUS & TRAPEZOID BODY

Fig. 19.   Cross section of the lower region of the pons.

The medial lemniscus is seen as an elliptic mass extending transversely in contact with the basilar portion of the pons. The *medial longitudinal fasciculus* retains its position near the midline in the floor of the fourth ventricle. This fasciculus now contains the tectospinal and tectobulbar tracts, the vestibulomesencephalic tract and other, less important tracts.

The *trapezoid body* is a prominent band of decussating fibers in the ventral part of the tegmentum. Its fibers interlace at right angles with those of the medial lemniscus. The *superior olive* is a small oval nucleus which lies lateral and slightly dorsal to the trapezoid body. The *central tegmental tract* is an isolated bundle in the ventral part of the reticular formation descending to the inferior olivary nucleus from an undetermined source—possibly from the reticular substance of the midbrain. The nucleus and spinal root of the trigeminal nerve have not changed

40

their position, but they now are covered on the lateral side by the inferior and middle cerebellar peduncles.

Immediately dorsal to the superior olive, and medial to the nucleus of the spinal root of n. V, is the pear-shaped *motor nucleus of the facial nerve* (n. VII). Before leaving the brain stem, the fibers of the facial nerve form an internal loop (*genu of facial nerve*). The first leg of this loop courses dorsomedially toward the floor of the fourth ventricle passing close to, and just caudal to, the *nucleus of the abducent nerve*. The facial nerve circles medially around the abducent nucleus returning on the rostral side of the nucleus. After completing this hairpin bend, the nerve takes a direct course ventrolaterally and slightly caudally to its exit at the pontomedullary junction. Fibers of the abducent nerve take a course similar to those of the hypoglossal, passing close to the lateral border of the pyramidal tract to emerge on the ventral aspect of the brain stem.

Nuclei of the vestibular group continue to occupy the lateral area in the floor of the fourth ventricle. The individual sub-nuclei at this level are the *lateral* and *superior*, instead of the medial and spinal which are found in the medulla.

Paired cerebellar nuclei are generally observed in sections through the cerebellum in the lower level of the pons (Fig. 19). The nuclei are:

F *Nucleus fastigii*—located in midline of roof of fourth ventricle in the region of the vermis.
Afferent fibers—from flocculonodular lobe of cerebellum.
Efferent fibers—to vestibular nuclei over fastigiobulbar tract.

G *Nucleus globosus*—small group of cells located just lateral to above nucleus.
Afferent fibers—from the paleocerebellum.
Efferent fibers—to red nucleus over superior cerebellar peduncle.

E *Nucleus emboliformis*—slightly elongated cellular mass located between the globose and dentate nuclei.
Afferent and efferent fibers—similar to nucleus globosus.

D . *Nucleus dentatus*—is the largest and most lateral of the cerebellar nuclei. It is serrated in appearance, purse-like in shape with an anteromedian hilum.
Afferent fibers—from the paleo- and neocerebellar cortex.
Efferent fibers—to red nucleus and ventrolateral nucleus of the thalamus over the superior cerebellar peduncles.

*Middle Portion* (Fig. 20). The basilar portion is widened and thickened. The pyramidal tracts are now dispersed in separate fascicles. Mingling with them are numerous other scattered longitudinal fibers. These are the *corticopontile tracts* descending from the frontal, temporal, parietal, and occipital lobes to synapse with cells of the pontile nuclei.

Two oval-shaped nuclei lie side by side in the dorsolateral part of the tegmentum. The more lateral one is the *superior sensory nucleus of*

41

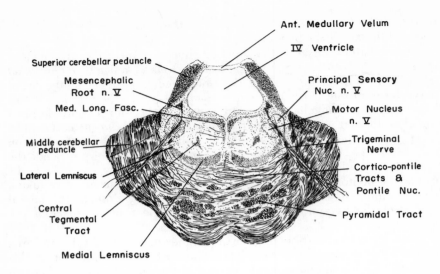

Fig. 20.  Cross section of the middle region of the pons.

*the trigeminal nerve;* the medial is the *motor nucleus* (masticator nucleus) *of the trigeminal nerve.* Small filaments of the nerve pass dorsally as the mesencephalic root of the trigeminal nerve. Trigeminal fibers emerging from the surface of the pons pass directly through the middle cerebellar peduncle in a ventrolateral direction.

The *superior cerebellar peduncles* (brachia conjunctiva) appear at the sides of the fourth ventricle as large compact bands. The anterior medullary velum forms the roof of the ventricle.

## MIDBRAIN

The midbrain is a short segment between the pons and the diencephalon. It is traversed by the *cerebral aqueduct*, an extraordinarily small tubular passage connecting the third ventricle with the fourth.

### External Markings of the Midbrain

*Ventral Aspect* (Fig. 13). The inferior surface is formed by two rope-like bundles of fibers, the *crura cerebri* and a deep *interpeduncular fossa* which separates them. Just before it disappears within the substance of the cerebral hemisphere above, each peduncle is skirted by the *optic tract* (n. II). At its caudal end the peduncle passes directly into the basilar portion of the pons. The *oculomotor nerves* (n. III) take exit from the sides of the interpeduncular fossa and emerge on the surface at the transverse groove between the pons and the midbrain.

*Dorsal Aspect* (Fig. 15). The dorsal surface of the midbrain presents four rounded elevations—the *corpora quadrigemina.* The rostral

42

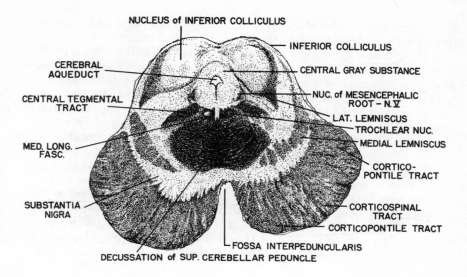

Fig. 21. Cross section of the lower region of the midbrain.

pair of swellings are the *superior colliculi*; the somewhat smaller, caudal pair are the *inferior colliculi*. The *trochlear nerves* (n. IV)—smallest of the cranial nerves—emerge from the dorsal surface just behind the inferior colliculi.

## Internal Structures of the Midbrain

In cross sections three zones are designated: (1) a basal portion, or *basis pedunculi*, which is synonymous to the crura cerebri; (2) the *tegmentum*, similar to the pontile tegmentum, and (3) the *tectum*, or roof portion, lying above the aqueduct and forming the quadrigeminal plate.

*Lower Half of the Midbrain* (Fig. 21). Each crus cerebri appears, in cross section, as a prominent, crescent-shaped mass of fibers within which the pyramidal tract occupies a central position, flanked at either side by corticopontile fibers. A brown-pigmented area of gray matter, known as the *substantia nigra*, lies between the peduncles and the tegmentum.

The central part of the tegmentum contains a massive interlace of fibers—the *decussation of the superior cerebellar peduncle*. The medial lemniscus is displaced laterally and rotated slightly. Its outer border is in close relation to adjacent fibers of the lateral spinothalamic tract. The *lateral lemniscus*, containing ascending fibers of the special sensory path of hearing, is clearly defined in the lateral part of the tegmentum dorsal to the lateral spinothalamic tract. The small, globular *nucleus of the trochlear nerve* lies near the medial longitudinal fasciculus in the ventral part of the central gray substance. An area of gray matter, the *nucleus of the inferior colliculus*, underlies each colliculus in the tectal region.

43

*Upper Half of the Midbrain* (Fig. 22). The cerebral peduncles and the substantia nigra continue to occupy the basal portion.

The red nuclei are conspicuous globular masses in the ventral portion of the tegmentum. The crossed fibers of the superior cerebellar peduncle pass into this nucleus and around its edges. Many of them terminate in the red nucleus; others pass forward to the thalamus. The *tectospinal* and *rubrospinal* tracts arise from this part of the midbrain. Both tracts cross near their origin—the tectospinal in the *dorsal tegmental decussation* (fountain decussation of Meynert); the rubrospinal in the *ventral tegmental decussation* (decussation of Forel).

The nuclear complex of the oculomotor nerve lies in the ventral part of the central gray matter with the medial longitudinal fasciculus beside it. The root fibers of the oculomotor nerve stream through and around the red nucleus before converging at their exit in the interpeduncular fossa.

The medial geniculate bodies may appear as projections on the lateral surfaces of the midbrain. They are auditory sensory relay centers, properly considered to be a part of the thalamus.

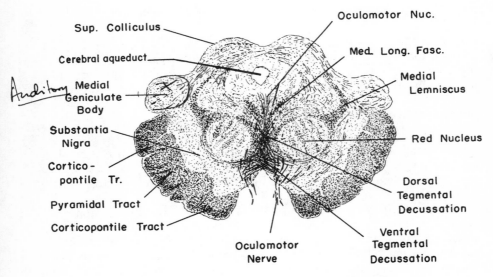

Fig. 22.   Cross section of the upper region of the midbrain.

44

## CHAPTER 9

# Functional Components
# of the Cranial Nerves

The function of the nerves of the body may be conveniently categorized by the following method. The fibers which innervate the body wall are designated as *somatic*. The fibers which innervate the viscera are termed *visceral*. Sensory fibers are designated as *afferent*, while the motor fibers are classified as *efferent*. The cranial nerves which have a function similar to that exhibited by the spinal nerves are classified as *general*. The cranial nerves which have specialized functions, such as supplying the eye and ear, conveying the olfactory and gustatory impulses or innervating the branchiomeric muscles, are classified as *special*.

The above criteria sometimes result in questionable classification. In these cases, custom has precedence and reasons for the choice become apparent.

## Résumé of Functional Components

A. General afferent fibers
   Are the sensory fibers which have their cells of origin in the craniospinal ganglia.

1. *Somatic afferent* (GSA)
   Includes the fibers which carry the exteroceptive (pain, temperature, touch, etc.) and the proprioceptive impulses from sensory endings in the body wall, tendons, joints, etc.
2. *Visceral afferent* (GVA)
   Are the fibers that carry sensory impulses (generally pain) from the visceral structures within the body.

B. Special afferent fibers
   This category is found only in the cranial nerves.

1. *Somatic afferent* (SSA)
   Consists of the nerves which carry the sensory impulses from the special sense organs, the ear and the eye (vision, hearing and equilibrium).
2. *Visceral afferent* (SVA)
   Consists of the fibers which are concerned with the specialized olfactory and gustatory receptors. These fibers are designated as visceral because of the functional association of the sensation with the digestive tract.

45

C. General efferent fibers
   Consists of the motor fibers which innervate the musculature of
   the body (except the branchiomeric fibers).

   1. *Somatic efferent* (SE)
      Consists of the fibers which convey the motor impulse to the
      somatic skeletal muscle (myotomic origin). The bulk of the
      fibers in the ventral root of the spinal nerve are of this type.
   2. *Visceral efferent* (GVE)
      Consists of the autonomic fibers which innervate smooth and
      cardiac muscle fibers and regulate glandular secretion. This
      category, which may be subdivided into the sympathetic and
      parasympathetic systems, is found in the spinal nerves and
      some cranial nerves.

D. Special efferent fibers
   Consists of the cranial nerves which innervate a specialized area
   of the skeletal musculature.

   1. *Visceral efferent* (SVE)
      This category includes the nerve components which innervate
      the skeletal muscles derived from the visceral arch mesoderm.
      These fibers are not a part of the autonomic nervous system.

## The Anatomical Position of Cranial Nerve Nuclei in the Brain Stem

The lateral walls of the embryonic brain and cord are demarcated
into an alar and a basal lamina by the appearance of the sulcus limitans
early in development. The nuclei in the basal plate, which are motor,
differentiate slightly earlier than the sensory nuclei located in the alar
plate. The localization of the various cranial nerve nuclei are indicated
and labelled according to their function (Fig. 23).

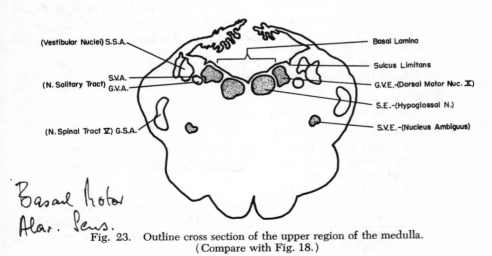

Basal Motor
Alar. Sens.

Fig. 23.   Outline cross section of the upper region of the medulla.
(Compare with Fig. 18.)

46

The somatic efferent fibers of the cranial nerves III, IV, VI, and XII arise from nuclei which are arranged as a discontinuous column of cells in the floor of the basal plate adjacent to the midline. The general visceral efferent nuclei will be observed to occupy a position lateral to the somatic efferent column. The motor nuclei of cranial nerves V, VII, IX, X, and XI, which provide the innervation of the branchiomeric musculature and are designated as the special visceral efferent nuclei, form the most lateral discontinuous column of neurons derived from the basal lamina.

The sensory fibers terminate in nuclei which are located in the alar lamina. The figure indicates that the special somatic afferent fibers terminate in the dorsalmost portion of the alar plate. The visceral afferent fibers terminate in a nuclear area adjacent to the visceral efferent column. The nucleus of the tractus solitarius serves as the receptor site —the cephalic portion of the nucleus receives the gustatory fiber terminals. The general somatic afferent column extends from the midbrain to the caudal extent of the medulla. It is subdivided into the mesencephalic nucleus, the main sensory nucleus and the nucleus of the spinal tract, all being parts of the trigeminal nerve. It will be noticed that the latter nucleus, that of the spinal tract, is continuous with the substantia gelatinosa and the dorsolateral fasciculus. The latter cord and cranial components have the same function—pain and temperature reception.

The cranial nerves, upon their entrance into the brain stem, subdivide into a variable number of fibers which make connections with their respective nuclei. For example, the nucleus ambiguus is the site of origin of the special visceral efferent fibers for the IX, X and the bulbar portion of the XI cranial nerves. Likewise, the central processes of the gustatory fibers of the cranial nerves VII, IX and X synapse with neurons in the cephalic portion of the nucleus of the tractus solitarius.

## An Outline of the Functional Components in the Cranial Nerves

1. Olfactory nerve *SVA*

   *Special visceral afferent*—the fila from the bipolar olfactory epithelial cells constitute the olfactory nerve.

2. Optic nerve *SSA*

   *Special somatic afferent*—the fibers which arise from the ganglion cells of the retina constitute the so-called nerve. It is not a true nerve but represents an evaginated fiber tract of the diencephalon. The fibers from the nasal halves of the retina decussate in the optic chiasma.

3. Oculomotor nerve *GSE*

   *Somatic efferent*—the fibers arise in the oculomotor nucleus and innervate the ⟨extrinsic⟩ muscles of the eye—except the superior oblique and the ~~lateral~~ rectus.

$$(LR_6 \ SO_4)_3$$

47

*General visceral efferent*—consists of the preganglionic fibers which arise in the accessory oculomotor (Edinger-Westphal) nucleus and terminate in the ciliary ganglion.

*General somatic afferent*—consists of the proprioceptive fibers for the extrinsic muscles innervated by the third nerve. These fibers are believed to terminate in the mesencephalic nucleus of the trigeminal nerve.

4. Trochlear nerve

*Somatic efferent*—fibers arise in the trochlear nucleus and innervate the superior oblique muscle of the eye.

*General somatic afferent*—consists of the proprioceptive fibers from the superior oblique muscle. Termination is unknown (possibly in the mesencephalic nucleus of the trigeminal nerve).

5. Trigeminal nerve

*General somatic afferent*—

Exteroceptive fibers—sensory fibers from the skin of the face and scalp and the ectodermal mucous membranes of the head (mouth and nasal chamber). The cells of origin are located in the semilunar ganglion.

Proprioceptive fibers—sensory fibers from the muscles of mastication and the other muscles innervated by the mandibular nerve. The cells of origin are located in the mesencephalic nucleus of the trigeminal nerve.

*Special visceral efferent*—fibers from the motor nucleus of the fifth nerve via the portio minor and mandibular nerve which innervate the muscles of mastication, tensor veli palati, tensor tympani, mylohyoid and the anterior belly of the digastric. These muscles arise from the first visceral arch.

6. Abducens nerve

*Somatic efferent*—fibers which arise in the abducens nucleus innervate the lateral rectus muscle of the eye.

*General somatic afferent*—consists of the proprioceptive fibers from the lateral rectus muscle. Termination is unknown, but probably similar to that of the trochlear nerve.

7. Facial nerve

*General visceral afferent*—fibers have cells of origin in the geniculate ganglion. The peripheral fibers receive the sensations of deep sensibility from the face. The fibers are a component of the nervus intermedius.

*Special visceral afferent*—cells of origin in the geniculate ganglion. Peripheral fibers terminate in the taste buds on the anterior two-thirds of the tongue. The fibers reach the tongue by way of the intermediate nerve, chorda tympani and lingual nerve. Central branches terminate in the rostral portion of the nucleus solitarius.

48

*General visceral efferent*—are the preganglionic fibers which arise in the superior salivatory nucleus. Synapse with the postganglionic neurons in the pterygopalatine and the submandibular ganglia. Preganglionic fibers are a component of the nervus intermedius.

*Special visceral efferent*—fibers arise from neurons in the motor nucleus of the seventh nerve. They innervate the superficial muscles of the face and scalp, the platysma, stylohyoid and the posterior belly of the digastric. These muscles originate from the second visceral arch.

8. Stato-acoustic nerve

*Special somatic afferent*

Exteroceptive fibers—cochlear nerve has bipolar cells of origin in the spiral ganglion. Peripheral processes receive stimuli from the hair cells in the cochlear duct. The central processes terminate in the cochlear nuclei.

Proprioceptive—vestibular nerve has bipolar cells of origin in the vestibular ganglion. Peripheral processes receive stimuli from hair cells in maculae and cristae. The central processes terminate in vestibular nuclei.

9. Glossopharyngeal nerve

*General visceral afferent*—the cell bodies, located in the inferior ganglion, have peripheral fibers which carry general sensory fibers from the posterior third of the tongue. and the pharynx. The central processes terminate in the nucleus of the solitary tract.

*Special visceral afferent*—the cell bodies of the same ganglion have peripheral fibers which carry the gustatory sense from the posterior third of the tongue. Central processes terminate in the rostral portion of the nucleus of the solitary tract.

*General visceral efferent*—preganglionic fibers from cells in the inferior salivatory nucleus terminate in the otic ganglion. Postganglionic fibers of the ganglion innervate the parotid gland.

*Special visceral efferent*—fibers originating from neurons in the nucleus ambiguus innervate the skeletal muscle of the third visceral arch (stylopharyngeus).

10. Vagus nerve

*General somatic afferent*—neurons, located in the superior ganglion, have fibers conveying exteroceptive sensations via the auricular nerve.

*General visceral afferent*—cell bodies, located in the inferior ganglion, have fibers conveying exteroceptive sensations from the viscera (pharynx, larynx and thoracic and abdominal viscera).

*Special visceral afferent*—peripheral processes of neurons in the inferior ganglion receive gustatory stimuli from epiglottal taste buds by way of the internal laryngeal nerve. .

*General visceral efferent*—preganglionic fibers from neurons in the dorsal motor nucleus of X innervate the thoracic and abdominal viscera (glands, cardiac muscle and smooth muscle—to the level of the splenic flexure of the colon). It will be remembered that the postganglionic neurons are located in the visceral walls.

*Special visceral efferent*—fibers from cells in the nucleus ambiguus innervate the skeletal musculature of the remaining visceral arches (soft palate, larynx and pharnyx).

11. Spinal Accessory nerve

*General somatic afferent*—proprioceptive fibers from the skeletal muscles innervated by this nerve. The cells of origin, located in the upper cervical spinal ganglia, reach the muscles via branchings of the cervical plexus.

*General visceral efferent*—are the fibers which arise in the dorsal motor nucleus of X to rejoin the vagus nerve. Believed to form components of the cardiac branches of the vagus nerve.

*Special visceral efferent*—a. Fibers arising from neurons in the nucleus ambiguus accompany those of the vagus nerve. Supply the skeletal musculature, in part, of the pharynx and larynx. b. A second group of fibers, which have their origin from neurons in the anterior gray horn of the cervical spinal cord, innervate the sternocleidomastoid and trapezius muscles.

12. Hypoglossal nerve

*Somatic efferent*—fibers which arise from neurons in the hypoglossal nucleus innervate the skeletal musculature of the tongue.

*General somatic afferent*—proprioceptive fibers from the lingual musculature (similar to that proposed for cranial nerves III, IV and VI). Scattered neurons, which have been found along the nerve, have been postulated to be the ganglion cells which serve this function.

Note: The nervus terminalis has been omitted from the summary. This cranial nerve has been studied primarily in the lower vertebrates.

## CHAPTER 10

7, 9, 10, 11, 12
12, 11, 9, 10, 7

# Cranial Nerves of the Medulla

## THE HYPOGLOSSAL NERVE (NERVE XII)

The hypoglossal nerve is the motor nerve of the tongue musculature. Its somatic efferent fibers are lower motor neuron fibers originating in cells of the hypoglossal nucleus. Among the muscles supplied by the hypoglossal nerve are the genioglossi which, by their posterior fibers, draw the root of the tongue forward and cause the tip of the tongue to protrude. Hemiparalysis, or hemiparesis, of the tongue results in unbalanced action of the genioglossus muscles. Consequently, on voluntary protrusion, the tongue deviates to the paralyzed side.

## THE ACCESSORY NERVE (NERVE XI)

The accessory nerve has two distinct parts. The spinal root, which arises from anterior horn cells of cervical cord segments one through five, ascends through the foramen magnum and courses along the side of the medulla. Here it joins the bulbar root from the medulla. After accompanying the spinal root fibers for a short distance, the bulbar fibers turn away to join the vagus nerve and are distributed with the terminal branches of the vagus. The spinal portion of nerve XI (special visceral efferent fibers) passes through the jugular foramen and descends in the neck to end in the sternomastoid and trapezius muscles. The spinal division of the accessory is, in reality, a displaced loop of the cervical plexus and not a true cranial nerve.

## THE VAGUS NERVE COMPLEX
## (NERVES IX, X, AND PORTIONS OF NERVES VII, XI)

Four nerves of the medulla are closely related in functions and in the configuration of their nuclear groups: (1) the nervus intermedius, the sensory and parasympathetic division of the facial nerve (n. VII); (2) the glossopharyngeal nerve (n. IX); (3) the vagus nerve (n. X); and (4) the bulbar portion of the accessory nerve (n. XI). These will be considered collectively as the vagal system..

### Course and Distribution of the Nerves of the Vagal System

*The Nervus Intermedius*

*pa A.*

The nervus intermedius, the smaller of two divisions of the facial nerve, enters the internal acoustic meatus and proceeds laterally in the facial canal toward the medial wall of the middle ear cavity. The sensory ganglion (geniculate ganglion) is located at the angle of a sharp bend in the canal. From this point some fibers of the nerve continue as the great superficial petrosal nerve to the pterygopalatine ganglion. The rest of the nervus intermedius starts downward in the facial canal, but leaves it abruptly and crosses the tympanic cavity as the chorda tympani. Leaving the middle ear at the inner end of the petro-tympanic fissure, the chorda tympani descends between the pterygoid muscles to join the lingual branch of the mandibular nerve. Some fibers of the chorda tympani are given off to the submandibular ganglion; the rest are distributed to taste receptors in the anterior two-thirds of the tongue.

## The Glossopharyngeal Nerve

The glossopharyngeal nerve leaves the skull through the jugular foramen at which point its two sensory ganglia, the superior and inferior, are located. The nerve passes downward and forward upon the surfaces of the stylopharyngeus and constrictor pharyngeus muscles to be distributed to the mucosa of the palatine tonsil, the fauces, and to the posterior one-third of the tongue.

Branches of the glossopharyngeal nerve:

*Tympanic* (Jacobson's nerve): enters the tympanic plexus and proceeds as the lesser superficial petrosal nerve to the otic ganglion.

*Carotid*: descends along the internal carotid artery to end in the carotid sinus and the carotid body.

*Pharyngeal*: enters the pharyngeal plexus with the vagus nerve and contributes motor fibers to the striated muscles of the pharynx.

*Stylopharyngeal*: to the stylopharyngeus muscle.

*Lingual*: sends taste and general sensory fibers to the posterior third of the tongue.

## The Vagus Nerve

The two sensory ganglia of the vagus nerve, the superior (jugular) and inferior (nodose), are located near the jugular foramen, through which the nerve passes. The nerve courses vertically down the neck in the carotid sheath and enters the thorax, passing anterior to the subclavian artery on the right and anterior to the aortic arch on the left. Both nerves pass behind the roots of the lungs. The left nerve continues on the ventral side, the right on the dorsal side of the esophagus to reach the gastric plexus. Fibers diverge to the duodenum, liver, biliary ducts, spleen, kidneys, and to the small and large intestine as far as the splenic flexure.

52

Branches of the vagus nerve:

*Auricular:* to skin in the external auditory canal and a small sector of the pinna (the central connections of this branch may be to the trigeminal system).

*Pharyngeal:* to the pharyngeal plexus, along with the glossopharyngeal nerve. Is the chief motor nerve of pharynx and soft palate.

*Superior laryngeal:* internal branch is sensory to mucosa of larynx and epiglottis; external branch innervates inferior pharyngeal constrictor and cricothyroid muscles.

*Recurrent laryngeal:* on the left side the nerve loops around the aortic arch from before backwards; on the right it takes a similar course around the subclavian artery. Both nerves ascend in the laryngotracheal grooves and supply motor fibers to the intrinsic muscles of the larynx and sensory fibers to the mucosa below the vocal cords.

*Cardiac* (superior and inferior cervical cardiac rami and thoracic branches): enter the cardiac plexus on the wall of the heart with cardiac nerves from the sympathetic trunks.

*Pericardial, bronchial, esophageal* and *other branches* (through the celiac and superior mesenteric plexi to the abdominal viscera).

## The Bulbar Accessory Nerve

The bulbar accessory nerve is joined with the vagus nerve and forms a portion of the pharyngeal branches.

## The Motor Portion of the Vagal System

The vagal system contains special visceral motor, parasympathetic, and sensory fibers but there is no separation of bundles into dorsal and ventral nerve roots as in the spinal nerves. All fibers enter and leave the medulla in a series of rootlets arranged in a longitudinal row dorsal to the olive (Fig. 24).

The cells of the nucleus ambiguus are lower motor neurons. Their axons enter the glossopharyngeal and vagus nerves to furnish the motor innervation of the striated musculature of the soft palate, the pharynx, and the larynx (Fig. 24).

Lower motor neuron lesions of the vagal system may cause difficulty in swallowing (dysphagia); regurgitation of fluids through the nose; difficulty in producing vocal sounds (dysphonia); and development of a nasal quality of consonant sounds (dysarthria). Unilateral paralysis of the vagus nerve produces flattening of the palatal arch on that side, and on phonation the uvula is drawn to the non-paralyzed side. One of the recurrent nerves may be injured inadvertently during operations on the thyroid gland resulting in transient or permanent hoarseness. Paralysis of both recurrent nerves produces stridor and dyspnea which may necessitate tracheotomy.

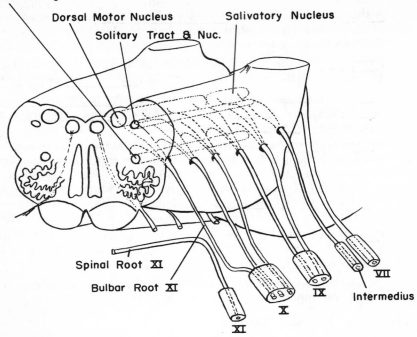

Nucleus Ambiguus

Dorsal Motor Nucleus

Salivatory Nucleus

Solitary Tract & Nuc.

Spinal Root XI

Bulbar Root XI

Intermedius

VII

IX

X

XI

Fig. 24. Attachments of the nervus intermedius (VII), the glossopharyngeal (IX), vagus (X), and bulbar accessory (XI) nerves to the upper portion of the medulla. The internal course of their motor, parasympathetic and sensory fibers is indicated.

## The Parasympathetic Portion of the Vagal System

The *dorsal motor nucleus of the vagus* consists of nerve cell bodies whose axons leave the medulla and are distributed to ganglia located in the head, neck, thorax, and abdomen. The ganglia are located close to the viscera which they innervate and they send short fibers directly to the smooth muscle and gland cells of these organs. The fibers that arise in the dorsal motor nucleus are referred to as preganglionic fibers; those proceeding from the ganglia to muscle and gland cells are postganglionic.

At the rostral end of the dorsal motor nuclear column is a group of neurons called the *salivatory nucleus* and activity of its cells stimulates secretion by the salivary glands. The cells in the *superior part* of the salivatory nucleus send their preganglionic fibers to the nervus intermedius, while those in the *inferior part* of the nucleus send preganglionic fibers to the glossopharyngeal nerve (Fig. 24). Some of the preganglionic fibers entering the nervus intermedius terminate in the pterygopalatine ganglion. This parasympathetic ganglion sends postganglionic fibers to the lacrimal gland and to the mucosal glands of the palate, pharynx, and posterior nasal chambers. Other preganglionic fibers of the nervus intermedius end in the submandibular ganglion which sends postganglionic fibers to the submandibular and sublingual salivary glands. Preganglionic fibers of the glossopharyngeal nerve end in the otic ganglion, the parasympathetic ganglion which innervates the parotid gland.

The dorsal motor nucleus furnishes the preganglionic fibers of the vagus nerve, the largest and most important parasympathetic nerve of the body. Ganglion cells receiving terminals of the vagus nerve are found in the autonomic plexuses of the walls of the cervical, thoracic and abdominal viscera. Stimulation of vagal parasympathetic fibers slows the heart rate; constricts the smooth muscle of the bronchial tree; stimulates the glands of the bronchial mucosa; promotes peristalsis in the gastrointestinal tract; relaxes the pyloric and ileocolic sphincters; and stimulates the secretion of gastric and pancreatic juices.

## The Sensory Portion of the Vagal System

The sensory fibers of the vagus and glossopharyngeal nerves have their cell bodies in the sensory ganglia which are attached to these nerves near the base of the skull. The geniculate ganglion, located at the external genu of the facial nerve, contains the cell bodies of the sensory fibers of the nervus intermedius. After entering the medulla in the dorsolateral sulcus, all sensory fibers of the vagal system pass directly into the solitary tract. The fibers turn in a caudal direction and give off terminal branches to the nucleus of the solitary tract as they descend (Fig. 24).

The sense of taste, initiated by chemical stimulation of special receptor cells in the taste buds of the tongue, is carried to the rostral portion of the solitary tract by sensory fibers of the nervus intermedius and the glossopharyngeal nerves. The nervus intermedius, through its chorda tympani branch, receives the gustatory stimuli from the anterior two-thirds of the tongue; the glossopharyngeal, from the posterior one-third. A small number of taste buds located on the epiglottis receive innervation from the vagus nerve. Secondary fibers from the nucleus of the solitary tract are presumed to cross and ascend to the thalamus. Thalamic fibers go to a cortical area for taste recognition located in the opercular part of the postcentral gyrus.

The glossopharyngeal and vagus nerves supply the afferent fibers of touch and pain senses to the mucosa of the posterior part of the soft palate, auditory tube, pharynx, larynx, and trachea. Touch fibers, whose nerve cell bodies are in the sensory ganglia of these nerves, enter the solitary tract along with the special sensory fibers of taste. Most of the touch fibers from this area are contained in the vagus nerve. Pain stimuli from the region of the pharynx are carried in the glossopharyngeal nerve, but after reaching the brain stem, these fibers descend in the spinal root of the trigeminal nerve instead of passing to the solitary tract.

The vagus nerve also conducts sensory stimuli from the heart, bronchi, esophagus, stomach, small intestine, and ascending colon. Vagal stimulation may be responsible for the indescribable, unpleasant sensation of nausea, but otherwise, afferent impulses from viscera are not

55

recognized consciously when they are conducted by the vagal route. Visceral pain is transmitted by the lateral spinothalamic tracts of the spinal cord. The chief function of the non-taste, afferent fibers of the vagal system concerns the operation of visceral reflexes.

## Reflexes of the Vagal System

### The Salivary-Taste Reflex

The secretory function of the vagal system is illustrated by the salivary-taste reflex. When a drop of weak acid is placed on the tongue, the salivary glands increase their output of saliva. The afferent stimulus is carried to the nucleus of the solitary tract by taste fibers. Connecting fibers from this nucleus go to the salivatory nuclei, stimulating parasympathetic neurons which supply the salivary glands.

### The Carotid Sinus Reflex

Increased pressure of the blood stream stimulates special receptors in the wall of the carotid sinus and sends impulses over fibers of the glossopharyngeal nerve to the solitary tract. Connections from the solitary tract, or its nucleus, to the dorsal motor nucleus completes a reflex arc which slows the heart rate. Simultaneously, other reflex connections are made to a diffuse vasomotor center located in the reticular formation of the medulla. Inhibition of the vasomotor center,. whose fibers descend to sympathetic neurons of the spinal cord, produces vasodilation of peripheral blood vessels and further reduces the blood pressure. Some individuals with hypersensitive carotid sinus reflexes are subject to attacks of syncope brought on by light external pressure over the sinus.

### The Carotid Body Reflex

The carotid body contains special chemoreceptors which respond to changes in the carbon dioxide and oxygen content of the circulating blood. Stimulation is carried to the solitary tract by the glossopharyngeal nerve. Fibers then go to the respiratory center of the medulla where they influence the rate of respiration. The respiratory center consists of diffusely arranged cells of the reticular formation with reticulospinal fibers descending to the lower motor neurons of the phrenic and intercostal nerves.

Propagation of nerve impulses over the reticulospinal fibers of the respiratory center produces inspiration. As the lungs become inflated, stretch receptors in the walls of bronchioles discharge impulses which ascend to the medulla through the vagus nerve. Connecting neurons reach the respiratory center and, by inhibition, temporarily arrest the inspiratory phase of respiration. The respiratory center is dependent on impulses descending from the hypothalamus for maintenance of the rhythm. The voluntary motor system can control respiration but is not essential.

## The Cough Reflex *Vagus*

Coughing is usually a response to irritation of the mucosa of the larynx, trachea, or bronchial tree, but it may also be produced, at times, by irritation of vagus nerve fibers in other locations including the fibers that supply the external auditory canal or the tympanic membrane. Afferent impulses reach the solitary tract by way of the vagus nerve. Connections are made to the respiratory center to bring about forced expiration. At the same time fibers going to the nucleus ambiguus cause efferent impulses to descend to the muscles of the larynx and pharynx.

## The Gag Reflex *9*

Touching the posterior wall of the pharynx is followed by constriction and elevation of the pharynx. The afferent fibers for this reflex are sensory fibers of the glossopharyngeal nerve. After entering the solitary tract, synaptic connections are made with the nucleus ambiguus which sends efferent fibers to the striated muscles of the pharynx.

## The Vomiting Reflex *10*

Forceful emptying of the stomach is brought about by relaxation of the cardiac sphincter and reversed peristalsis, assisted by contraction of muscles of the abdomen and thorax. At the same time, inspiration is arrested by closure of the glottis. The stimulus, which may arise in any part of the gut innervated by the vagus is sent to the nucleus of the solitary tract by sensory fibers of the vagus nerve. From here, impulses go to the dorsal motor nucleus, to initiate the parasympathetic responses, and to the nucleus ambiguus to close the glottis. The diaphragm and the abdominal muscles are recruited by impulses which descend from the reticular formation of the medulla to reach the appropriate lower motor neurons in the spinal cord.

A general elevation of intracranial pressure often causes vomiting, and it may also occur if there is localized pressure on the medulla.

## CHAPTER 11

# Cranial Nerves of the Pons
# and Midbrain

## THE ABDUCENT NERVE (NERVE VI)

The abducent nerve, arising from its nucleus beneath the fourth ventricle in the pons, supplies the motor fibers of the *lateral rectus muscle* of the eye. Leaving the brain stem ventrally, at the junction of the medulla and pons, the nerve passes along the floor of the posterior fossa of the skull to reach the lateral wall of the cavernous sinus. Prolonged elevation of intracranial pressure, from any cause, may damage the abducent nerve by compression. Complete unilateral destruction of the abducent nerve makes it impossible to turn the eye outward. The unopposed pull of the medial rectus muscle causes the eye to turn inward and produces *internal strabismus*, or internal squint. Since images do not fall on corresponding points of the left and right retinae, they cannot be properly fused. The result is *diplopia* or double vision, which the patient seeks to minimize by turning the head to one side. Weakness of one external rectus muscle may only become apparent when the patient attempts to turn the eyes to one side and is unable to move the affected eye lateral to the mid-position. With bilateral abducent nerve paralysis neither eye can be moved in a lateral direction past the mid-position.

## THE TROCHLEAR NERVE (NERVE IV)

The *nucleus of the trochlear nerve* is located ventral to the *central gray matter* in the region of the inferior colliculus. The fibers of the nerve descend slightly and curve around the central gray matter. The fibers decussate and make their exit from the dorsal surface of the tectum caudal to the inferior colliculus. The trochlear nerve innervates the *superior oblique muscle*. Isolated lesions of the trochlear nerve are uncommon and the symptoms are inconspicuous. The ability to turn the eye outward and downward is impaired.

## THE OCULOMOTOR NERVE (NERVE III)

The *nucleus of the oculomotor nerve* is located ventral to the central gray matter in the region of the superior colliculus. The fibers course ventrally, some penetrating the lateral portion of the *red nucleus* and the medial portion of the *cerebral peduncle*. After its exit from the brain stem at the interpeduncular fossa, the nerve passes close to the arteries

58

*ciliary muscle - accommodation.*
*sphincter M. of Iris - constricts pupil*

of the circulus arteriosus which is an anastomotic circuit at the base of the brain. An aneurysm (saccular dilation) of one of the arteries in this region may compress the oculomotor nerve. Tumor or hemorrhage may force the inferior margin of the temporal lobe of the cerebrum under the edge of the tentorium cerebelli and exert pressure on the oculomotor nerve as it crosses the tentorium beside the dorsum sellae of the sphenoid bone.

The oculomotor nerve innervates the *medial, superior* and *inferior* *M, S, I* *recti,* the *inferior oblique,* and the *levator palpebrae superioris.* It also *recti* supplies the preganglionic parasympathetic fibers for the *ciliary ganglion* *inf. oblique* whose postganglionic fibers innervate the *ciliary muscle* for accommo- *Lp. sup.* dation and the *sphincter muscle of the iris* which constricts the pupil.

Complete paralysis of the oculomotor nerve results in: (1) outward deviation of the eye (*external strabismus*) and loss of ability to turn the eye inward; (2) *ptosis*, or drooping of the upper eyelid, with loss of ability to raise the lid voluntarily; and (3) dilation of the pupil (*mydriasis*) because of the unopposed action of the radial muscle fibers of the iris. Incomplete lesions produce partial effects. There may be some weakness of all functions, or one symptom may appear without the others, e.g., dilation of the pupil without paralysis of eye movements.

The upper motor neurons which descend as the corticomesencephalic portion of the pyramidal system to motor nuclei of nerves III, IV and VI cross in the pons and make connections with all three nuclei to bring about cooperative, or conjugate, movements of both eyes. Upper motor lesions therefore do not affect one nerve without involving the others. The cortex of the left frontal lobe controls voluntary deviation of the eyes to the right. Destructive lesions above the crossing of the corticomesencephalic tract cause loss of the ability to turn the eyes voluntarily to the side opposite the lesion. Following such a lesion the predominating influence of the unaffected corticomesencephalic tract may cause both eyes to be deviated to the side of the lesion so that the patient "looks at his lesion."

## THE FACIAL NERVE (NERVE VII)

*Stylomastoid foramen*
*Bell's palsy*

The motor division of the seventh cranial nerve is considered to be the facial nerve proper, its sensory and parasympathetic components (nervus intermedius) having been included with the vagal system. The facial is the motor nerve of all movements of facial expression. Through the action of the orbicularis oculi muscle, the facial nerve closes the eyelid and protects the eye.

The facial nerve proceeds from the pontocerebellar angle through the facial canal, leaves the skull by the stylomastoid foramen, and enters the substance of the parotid gland behind the ramus of the mandible where it divides into branches which fan out to all parts of the face and scalp.

An interruption of the facial nerve causes total paralysis. The muscles of one side of the face sag and the normal lines around the lips, nose and forehead are "ironed out." On attempting to smile, the corner of the mouth is drawn to the opposite side. Saliva may drip from the corner of

59

the mouth. The cheek may puff out in expiration because the buccinator muscle is paralyzed. The patient's inability to close his eyes leads to irritation and predisposes to infection, so it is advisable for him to wear an eye mask or to have the lids closed by sutures. It is not uncommon for the facial nerve to become paralyzed overnight without any known cause, a condition known as Bell's palsy. Fortunately most of these patients recover spontaneously in one or two months.

There are no stretch reflexes available for testing the superficial musculature of the face so these cannot serve as a point of distinction in upper motor neurons involving facial fibers of the corticobulbar tract. A supranuclear lesion of this type can usually be recognized by other means. Nearly all of the upper motor neurons going to those cells of the facial nucleus which supply the lower part of the face are crossed fibers; uncrossed as well as crossed fibers are sent to motor cells for the upper part of the face (Fig. 25). An upper motor neuron lesion therefore disconnects all of the voluntary control fibers for lower facial muscles, but leaves an uncrossed connection open for willed movements of the upper facial muscles. As a result the upper part of the face is spared from paralysis.

When paralysis is due to injury to upper motor neurons rather than to the facial nerve itself or its nucleus, involuntary contraction of the muscles of facial expression is still possible. By utilizing extrapyramidal circuits, a spontaneous grin may occur by utilizing muscles which cannot be moved voluntarily.

## THE TRIGEMINAL NERVE (NERVE V)

The trigeminal nerve is a mixed nerve with a large motor root supplying the muscles of mastication and an even larger sensory root distributed to the mouth, nasal cavity, orbit, and anterior one-half of the scalp.

### Motor Division of Nerve V

Fibers from the masticator, or motor nucleus, in the lateral tegmentum of the pons enter the mandibular branch of the fifth nerve and go to the temporalis, masseter, and medial and lateral pterygoid muscles. Peripheral lesions of this portion of the nerve cause atrophy and weakness which can be recognized by feeling the size and tautness of the masseter muscles as the jaws are clenched. Fasciculations may also be seen in the denervated muscle fibers. Owing to the action of the pterygoid muscles which draw the mandible forward and toward the midline, there is deviation of the chin in the direction of the paralyzed side when the jaws are opened. Each masticator nucleus receives upper motor neurons from both the left and the right motor areas of the cortex, and supranuclear lesions confined to one side do not produce any marked effects. The jaw jerk is a stretch reflex obtained by tapping the middle of the chin while the mouth is slightly open. The normal response, which is usually a minimal one becomes exaggerated after upper motor neuron lesions.

60

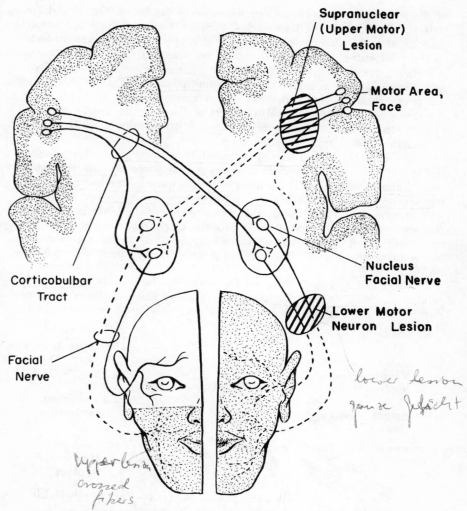

Fig. 25. The shaded areas of the face show the distribution of facial muscles paralyzed after a supranuclear lesion of the corticobulbar tract, and after a lower motor
neuron lesion of the facial nerve.

## Sensory Division of Nerve V   *pain + temp.*

The T-cells of the semilunar ganglion contain the cell bodies of the
afferent fibers of the fifth nerve with the unique exception of the proprioceptive fibers from neuromuscular spindles, whose cell bodies are in the
mesencephalic nucleus of the nerve. Pain and temperature fibers turn
caudally and form the spinal root of the trigeminal nerve, giving off terminal branches to the *nucleus of the spinal root V* as they descend
through the pons and medulla. Fibers arising from cells of the nucleus

61

of the spinal root cross to the opposite side of the brain stem in a diffuse pattern and ascend to the medial part of the posteromedial ventral nucleus of the thalamus from which thalamocortical fibers are projected to the postcentral gyrus. Similar crossing fibers are given off from the *principal sensory nucleus* (Fig. 26). The name "trigeminal lemniscus" is sometimes applied to all of the trigeminothalamic fibers, although they are never gathered into a distinct and separate bundle. In the medulla, the crossed pain and temperature fibers of the face are located near the medial lemniscus; as they reach the pons, they gradually shift laterally to join the lateral spinothalamic tract.

Lesions in the lateral part of the medulla or lower pons which damage the spinal root of the trigeminal nerve are likely to include the lateral spinothalamic tract also. This causes *alternating analgesia:* loss of pain and temperature sense on the same side of the face as the lesion, and loss of pain and temperature sense on the opposite side of the body beginning at the neck. In the upper pons and midbrain, the fibers of the pain-temperature and touch systems are all close together, and in these regions one lesion produces anesthesia of the opposite side of the body including the face.

When the cornea is touched by a foreign body, the corneal reflex produces prompt closing of the eyelids. Sensory fibers entering the upper part of the spinal root of the trigeminal nerve synapse with cells of the

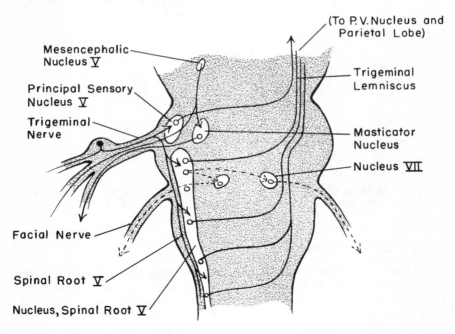

Fig. 26. Connections of the sensory and motor fibers of the trigeminal nerve within the brain stem from dorsal aspect. Circuits for the corneal reflexes are indicated by dotted lines. The nuclei are shown on one side for the sake of clarity.

nucleus of the spinal root which send axons to the nucleus of the facial nerve (Fig. 26). Motor fibers of the facial nerve then activate the orbicularis oculi muscle to close the eye. Connecting fibers go to both facial nuclei to close both eyes. The response on the side which is stimulated is the direct corneal reflex; that in the other eye is the consensual corneal reflex. Interrupting the trigeminal nerve abolishes both responses. A consensual but no direct reflex will be obtained if the ipsilateral facial nerve is destroyed; but at the same time, reflex connections are made with autonomic neurons to produce increased lacrimation.

Tic douloureux, or trigeminal neuralgia, is a disorder characterized by attacks of unbearably severe pain over the distribution of one or more branches of the trigeminal nerve. A small trigger zone, stimulation of which sets off one of the paroxysms, may be present. No cause for the disease has been discovered.

Lesion in last part of medulla or lower pons
 - gives alternating analgesia
  - loss of pain + temp same side of
  face + same side as lesion

Corneal reflex - test of V̄ + V̄II
 if blocked V̄ - no reflex

CHAPTER 12

# Hearing

**The Auditory System** ⑧ *(handwritten: Vestibular / Chochlear - hearing.)*

The eighth cranial nerve is the original sensory nerve of the semi-circular canals of fish—an effective mechanism for maintaining equilibrium and orientation in space.

The auditory organ, initially the lagena and then the cochlea, have been developed in the labyrinth of the land vertebrates. Because of this evolutionary change a new division of the eighth nerve appeared to serve the auditory function. Thus, the eighth nerve has two components—a vestibular and a cochlear division—so distinct in their function and anatomical relationship that they could almost be considered as separate cranial nerves.

The auditory apparatus has three components—the external, the middle, and the internal ear. The *tympanic membrane* of the external ear receives the airborne vibrations. The chain of three ossicles (*malleus, incus* and *stapes*) in the middle ear provides a lever which has a piston-like function and also amplifies the pressure applied at the *oval window*. The internal ear, or *cochlea*, is a tube resembling a snail shell, about 3.5 cm. long, and exhibiting 2½ turns. The central pillar or *modiolus* provides the bony support for the *bony spiral lamina* which partially divides the cochlea into two fluid filled (perilymph) chambers—the *scala vestibuli* and the *scala tympani*. The *basilar membrane* completes the separation of the scalae. A subdivision of the scala vestibuli is the *scala media* (cochlear duct) which is bordered by the *vestibular membrane* on the upper surface. The cochlear duct contains *endolymph* and is bordered by the *organ of Corti* which contains the sensory epithelium or the *hair cells*. The vibrations of the stapes are converted into pressure waves in the perilymph which travel through the scala vestibuli to the *helicotrema* (the apical connection between the vestibular and tympanic scalae) and down the scala tympani to be damped at the *round window*. The pressure waves cause a vibration of the basilar membrane which stimulates the hair cells of the organ of Corti. The hair cells serve as mechanoreceptors in which the mechanical energy (pressure waves) is transduced into a potential which is received by the closely applied dendritic processes of the spiral ganglion cells. The *spiral ganglion*, located in the modiolus of the cochlea, contains the bipolar cells of the cochlear division of the eighth nerve.

The organ of Corti serves as an audio-frequency analyzer. It has been determined that the highest tones (highest in pitch and frequency) maximally stimulate the hair cells in the most basal portion of the cochlea. The tones of lowest pitch maximally stimulate the most apical hair cells.

64

Tones or sounds in between stimulate the hair cells in the intermediate portion of the basilar membrane.

## The Auditory Pathway

The cochlear nerve enters the brain stem at the junction of the medulla and pons. As it attaches to the brain stem, the nerve clings to the lateral side of the inferior cerebellar peduncle and enters two nuclei, the *posterior* and *anterior cochlear nuclei*. The entering fibers of the nerve make synapses with cells of the cochlear nuclei, and the axons of these cells pass to the *lateral lemniscus* through which the auditory impulses ascend to the midbrain and thalamus. Many fibers cross to enter the lemniscus of the opposite side, but some go directly to the lemniscus of the same side. Crossing fibers from the anterior cochlear nucleus are more diffusely situated in the pontile tegmentum (Fig 27).

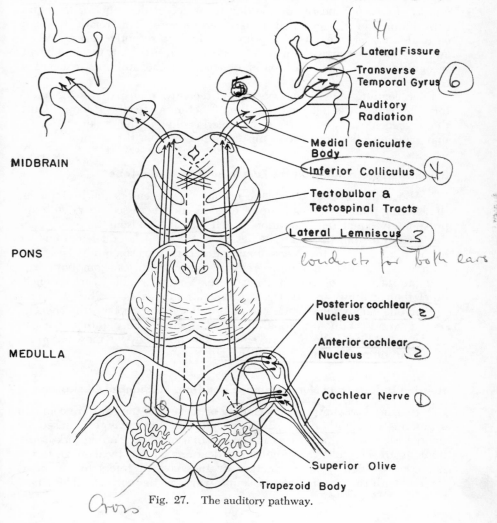

Fig. 27. The auditory pathway.

65

The *nucleus of the trapezoid body,* the *superior olive,* and the *nucleus of the lateral lemniscus* are special cell groups which lie along the path of auditory fibers as they proceed toward the midbrain (Fig. 27). Auditory fibers are given off to each of these nuclei. Some fibers from the nuclei re-enter the lateral lemniscus; others go to different locations to establish auditory reflex arcs. A few fibers of the lateral lemniscus pass directly to the medial geniculate body as the central acoustic tract; the rest of them terminate in the *nucleus of the inferior colliculus* which sends axons to the *medial geniculate* body through the *brachium of the inferior colliculus.*

The medial geniculate bodies are the final sensory relay stations of the hearing path, a special sensory nucleus of the thalamus. The efferent connection of the medial geniculate body to the temporal lobe forms the *auditory radiation* which goes to the *anterior transverse temporal gyrus* (*gyrus of Heschl*) located on the dorsal surface of the superior temporal convolution and partly buried in the lateral fissure. This relatively small cortical area, area 41, is the primary auditory receptive area. When auditory impulses arrive at area 41, a noise is "heard," but the intelligent recognition of a particular sound depends on the auditory associative cortex.

Descending fibers have been found recently in all parts of the auditory pathway. It is believed that they function as feedback loops. One, the olivocochlear bundle (from the superior olive to the organ of Corti), may have an inhibitory action on the impulses from the cochlea.

### Bilateral Representation of the Ears in Each Temporal Lobe

Above the level at which the cochlear nerve enters the brain stem, the hearing pathway is made up of crossed and uncrossed fibers with approximately equal representation. Each lateral lemniscus therefore conducts stimuli from both ears. A lesion of the right lateral lemniscus, or of the right anterior transverse temporal gyrus, stops some impulses from both ears, but does not interfere with other impulses from both ears going to the cortex of the left hemisphere. No appreciable hearing deficit, other than inability to localize directions of sounds, is produced. Deafness in one ear usually signifies trouble in the acoustic nerve, the cochlea, or the sound-conducting apparatus of that side. The eighth nerve can be damaged bilaterally by toxic effects of some drugs, the most notorious being streptomycin, quinine and aspirin.

### Hearing Defects from Nerve Damage and from Mechanical Obstruction

Hearing loss and tinnitus (ringing or roaring in the ear) are common symptoms of eighth nerve disorder, but they also may be caused by middle ear disease, or by wax in the external meatus. Tuning fork examinations are helpful in distinguishing deafness caused by damage to the nerve or cochlea from conduction deafness which refers to the interference with the transmission of sound waves to the cochlea. The *Rinné*

66

*test* compares the patient's ability to hear a vibrating fork by bone conduction and by air conduction. The base of the fork is placed over the mastoid process of the skull. When it can no longer be heard, it is removed and the tines are held in front of the ear. A normal person continues to hear by air conduction after bone conduction ceases. In nerve deafness both are diminished but air conduction remains better than bone conduction. In conduction deafness, bone conduction is better than air conduction. The *Weber test* is performed by placing the base of the fork on the midline of the skull and asking the patient which ear hears the louder sound. In conduction deafness the sound is heard better in the defective ear; in nerve deafness it seems louder in the normal ear. Electronic audiometers have an important role in testing hearing since pure tones may be used at controlled intensities. Receivers for both air and bone conduction are available. It is possible to graph the results of these tests on the right and left ear for both air and bone conduction. Conduction deafness is indicated by a reception impairment in the lower frequencies of pure tones in the air conduction test. In nerve deafness, tested in the same manner, the threshold deficit occurs in the reception of tones in the higher frequencies.

## Auditory Reflexes

Auditory reflexes are operated by side branches from the main auditory pathway. The *superior olive* sends a bundle of fibers to the vicinity of the nucleus of the abducent nerve which continues, through the medial longitudinal fasciculus, to the nuclei of the oculomotor and trochlear nerves. These connections bring about conjugate movements of the eyes in response to a sound. Other fibers from the *tectum* continue into the spinal cord as components of the *tectospinal tract*. These fibers terminate on lower motor neurons in the cord supplying the muscles of the body which respond to sound.

Rinne test: conduct. by bone + air
on mastoid process (air should be better)

Weber - fork at midline of skull (lower tones)
deafness in conduction - better heard =
deaf ear.

nerv deafness - louder in normal
ear
(higher tones)

## CHAPTER 13

# The Vestibular System

The vestibular part of the eighth nerve has its peripheral endings on the hair cells of the maculae of the utricle and saccule, and on the hair cells of the cristae in the ampullae of the three semicircular canals. The nerve furnishes afferent fibers for co-ordinated reflexes of the eyes, neck, and body for maintaining equilibrium in accordance with the posture and movement of the head.

### The Vestibular Nerve and Its Central Connections

Axons of bipolar cells of the vestibular ganglion pass through the internal auditory canal and reach the upper medulla in company with the cochlear nerve. Most of the fibers of the vestibular nerve end in four vestibular nuclei which are clustered in the lateral part of the floor of the fourth ventricle (Fig. 28):

*Medial* vestibular nucleus (of Schwalbe)
*Lateral* vestibular nucleus (of Deiter)
*Superior* vestibular nucleus (of Bechterew)
*Spinal* vestibular nucleus (descending, inferior)

The afferent fibers from the semicircular canals terminate in the medial and superior vestibular nuclei primarily, while those from the maculae terminate in the lateral and spinal nuclei. The canals respond to angular movements, while the utriculus and sacculus are concerned with gravitational motion (vertical motion).

A few fibers of the vestibular nerve pass directly to the cerebellum, ending in the cortex of the flocculonodular lobe. Connections are made within the cerebellum to the *nucleus fastigii* which gives rise to the *fastigiobulbar tract* (tract of Russell). The fibers of this tract terminate in the vestibular nuclei and on the hair cells of the labyrinth. As they pass from the cerebellum they loop around the superior cerebellar peduncle to form the *uncinate fasciculus*. The vestibular fibers which pass to and from the cerebellum lie on the medial side of the inferior cerebellar peduncle and constitute a portion of the peduncle sometimes referred to as *the juxtarestiform body*. An additional efferent component arises in the lateral vestibular nucleus primarily, which terminates on the vestibular hair cells. It is believed that the vestibular efferent pathways exhibit a central influence on the receptors of the membranous labyrinth.

### The Vestibulospinal Tracts

Two vestibulospinal tracts arise from the vestibular nuclei. The lateral tract (uncrossed) comes from the lateral vestibular nucleus; the

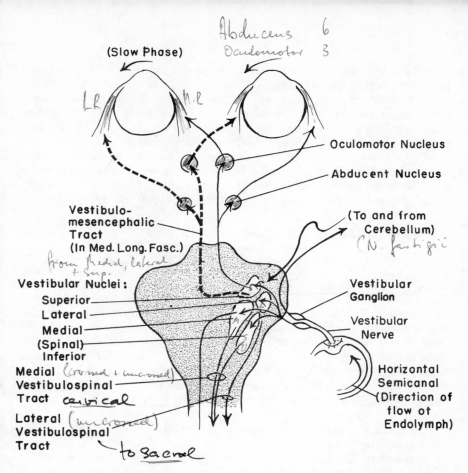

(Slow Phase)

*Abducens  6*
*Oculomotor  3*

*LR*     *M.R*

Oculomotor Nucleus

Abducent Nucleus

Vestibulo-
mesencephalic
Tract
(In Med. Long. Fasc.)
*from medial, lateral + sup.*

(To and from
Cerebellum)
*N. fastigii*

Vestibular Nuclei:
Superior
Lateral
Medial
(Spinal)
Inferior

Vestibular
Ganglion

Vestibular
Nerve

Medial *(crossed + uncrossed)*
Vestibulospinal
Tract  *cervical*

Lateral *(uncrossed)*
Vestibulospinal
Tract  *to sacral*

Horizontal
Semicanal
(Direction of
flow of
Endolymph)

Fig. 28.  Vestibular pathways. Nystagmus induced by centripetal flow of endolymph
in a horizontal semicanal is indicated. The dotted lines show the probable route of
activating stimuli.

medial tract (with both crossed and uncrossed fibers) comes chiefly from
the medial and spinal vestibular nuclei. The *lateral vestibulospinal tract*
extends to the sacral level of the cord. The *medial vestibulospinal tract*
extends through the cervical level ending on lower motor neurons in the
anterior horn. Impulses descending in these tracts assist the local
myotactic reflexes and reinforce the tonus of the extensor muscles of the
limbs, producing enough extra force to support the body against gravity
and maintain an upright posture.

An animal in which the brain stem has been transected at the midbrain displays decerebrate rigidity with the legs held stiffly in extension.
To produce decerebrate rigidity, there must be normal gravitational pull
on the maculae of the utricles, and the vestibular nuclei, vestibulospinal
tracts and dorsal roots must be intact. It is probable that decerebration
abolishes the effect of certain descending fiber tracts and allows tonic
labyrinthine reflexes to send a continuous discharge to the spinal cord

69

over the vestibulospinal tracts. Decerebrate rigidity in its fully developed form is rarely seen in humans. Changes in tonus somewhat similar to decerebrate rigidity may appear in the muscles of the legs after transverse injury of the thoracic portion of the spinal cord. Complete transverse lesions usually result in paraplegia in flexion with the legs held in a permanently flexed position. Paraplegia in extension, with rigidity of the extensor muscles of the legs, occurs after incomplete lesions which spare the anterior funiculi. However, it is not certain whether the increase in extensor tonus is due to vestibulospinal fibers or to reticulospinal fibers which are also located in the ventral part of the spinal cord.

### The Vestibulomesencephalic Tract

Fibers from the superior, lateral and medial vestibular nuclei are carried rostrally in the medial longitudinal fasciculus. These fibers constitute the *vestibulomesencephalic tract* which is distributed to the motor nuclei of cranial nerves supplying the ocular muscles that control the position of the eyes. Vestibular reflexes, in cooperation with certain reflexes of the optic system, enable the eyes to remain fixed on stationary objects while the head and body are moving. Turning the head slightly to the right causes a small flow of endolymph in the horizontal semicircular canals—directed to the left, because the fluid's inertia makes it lag behind the movement of the head. Vestibular impulses are sent to the abducent and oculomotor nuclei and the eyes are turned to the left the proper distance to keep the fields of vision unchanged.

In order to produce left conjugate deviation of the eyes, the stimuli must travel by both medial longitudinal fasciculi to the left abducent nucleus and to the right oculomotor nerve. Or, the impulses may ascend in one medial longitudinal fasciculus to the oculomotor nucleus which sends impulses to the opposite medial rectus muscle (Fig. 28).

### Vestibular Nystagmus

If stimulation of hair cells in the appropriate ampulla of the semicircular canal is persistent, the eyes draw slowly to the left until they reach a limit and then jerk quickly to the right. These movements are repeated in rapid succession producing tremor-like oscillations of the eyes known as nystagmus. The direction of nystagmus is designated according to the direction of the fast component, although this is opposite to the movement induced by stimulation from the semicircular canal. The mechanism responsible for the quick component of nystagmus is not understood, but it probably is self-contained within the vestibular nuclei.

A rotation test of nystagmus may be performed by whirling the subject in a revolving chair, the head being tilted forward 30 degrees to bring the horizontal canals parallel with the floor. Movement is stopped abruptly after ten or twelve turns. Momentum causes the endolymph to continue to flow in the direction in which the head had been turning even though the head is now stationary. The nystagmus which is in-

70

duced lasts about 30 seconds in normal individuals. If rotation has been to the left, endolymph flows to the left and the slow component of the nystagmus is to the left. Since the quick component is to the right, it is properly called "nystagmus to the right." With a special chair designed to rotate the subject in any plane it is possible to test each of the three semicircular canals individually.

Caloric, or thermal, tests of nystagmus permit the vestibular system of each side to be tested separately. The subject is usually seated with the head tilted backwards about 60 degrees to bring the horizontal semicircular canal into a vertical plane, then the external auditory canal is douched with cold or hot water. Hot water warms the endolymph in the semicircular canal and causes it to rise. Stimulation of hair cells by the current flowing past the ampulla produces nystagmus. With hot water in the right ear the current goes to the left and the nystagmus has its slow component to the left, quick to the right. If cold water is used, the current is reversed and nystagmus is in the opposite direction.

Irritation or destruction of the vestibule, vestibular nerve, or the vestibular nuclei commonly produces nystagmus and may also cause deviation of the eyes to one side. If the right vestibular nerve is severed, the influence of the remaining left vestibular apparatus is unbalanced and causes conjugate deviation of the eyes to the right. In a few weeks this effect is overcome by the compensating influence of voluntary and visual reflex circuits. The quick component of nystagmus produced by an irritative lesion is usually toward the side of the lesion, but at times it may be difficult to distinguish effects of irritation on one side from those of destruction on the other. Although horizontal nystagmus is the most common type, vertical or rotatory forms of nystagmus also occur. Nystagmus is not due to a disturbance of the vestibular system in every instance; some types are produced by injuries to the cerebral cortex, optic reflex pathways, the cerebellum or by toxic substances.

## Sensory Aspects of Vestibular Stimulation

Fiber connections from the vestibular nuclei to the thalamus and cerebral cortex have been postulated but not demonstrated. However, stimulation of the vestibular apparatus, whether by motion of the body or by artificial means, produces definite conscious effects which take the form of a false sense of motion. Vertigo is a sensation of whirling. The individual himself may have a subjective feeling of rotation, or it may seem to him that external objects are spinning around. Feelings of giddiness, faintness, lightheadedness, etc., may be vaguely described in somewhat similar terms, but they should not be mistaken for true vertigo. Meniere's syndrome is a disease of uncertain nature which is characterized by periodic attacks of severe vertigo, often accompanied by nausea and prostration. Tinnitus and impairment of hearing are included in the syndrome. Motion sickness during travel by air or sea is a familiar manifestation of prolonged and unusual stimulation of the vestibular apparatus.

CHAPTER 14

# The Cerebellum

The cerebellum is situated in the posterior cranial fossa. It is attached to the pons, medulla and midbrain by the cerebellar peduncles which lie at the sides of the fourth ventricle on the ventral aspect of the cerebellum. The *tentorium cerebelli*, a transverse fold of the dura mater, stretches horizontally over the superior surface of the cerebellum and separates it from the overlying occipital lobes of the cerebrum. The surface of the cerebellum is corrugated by numerous parallel folds known as *folia*. A layer of gray matter, the *cerebellar cortex*, covers the surface and encloses an internal core of white matter. Several masses of cells are buried within the white matter. The *dentate nucleus* is the largest of the *roof nuclei* of the cerebellum. The roof nuclei have been described previously (p. 41).

### Primary Subdivisions of the Cerebellum

For descriptive purposes the cerebellum is divided into two large lateral masses, the *cerebellar hemispheres,* which fuse near the midline with a narrow middle portion called the *vermis* because of its fancied resemblance to a worm. Detailed descriptions of the anatomical subdivisions of the hemispheres and vermis are complicated and inconsistent. To avoid confusion, it will be sufficient here to partition the entire cerebellum into three lobes:

1. The *flocculonodular lobe* consists of the paired *flocculi*, which are small appendages in the posterior inferior region, and the *nodulus,* which is the inferior part of the vermis (archicerebellum).
2. The *anterior lobe,* of modest size, is the portion of the cerebellum which lies anterior to the *primary sulcus* (paleocerebellum).
3. The *posterior lobe* is the larger, or main part, of the cerebellum and is located between the other two lobes.

The flocculonodular lobe represents the cerebellar portion of the vestibular system and, phylogenically, is the oldest part of the cerebellum. The anterior lobe, particularly its vermis portion, receives most of the proprioceptive impulses of the spinocerebellar pathway and is also an early developed area of the cerebellum. The flocculonodular and the anterior lobes are the predominant regions in the primitive vertebrates. The posterior lobe receives the cerebellar connections of the cerebrum and has become greatly expanded in the mammals which have developed an extensive cerebral cortex. The posterior lobe is frequently called the *neocerebellum* for this reason.

72

## The Peduncles of the Cerebellum

The three, paired cerebellar peduncles are composed of large numbers of fibers entering and leaving the cerebellum to connect it with other parts of the nervous system.  *I — Post. Spinocereb.*

The *inferior cerebellar peduncle* (restiform body) contains a single efferent tract, the fastigiobulbar, which goes to the vestibular nuclei and completes a vestibular circuit through the cerebellum. Afferent fibers are much more numerous. They reach the inferior cerebellar peduncle from four sources:

1. Fibers from the *vestibular nerve.*
2. *Olivocerebellar fibers* from the inferior olivary nuclei.
3. The *posterior spinocerebellar* tract from the spinal cord.
4. *Dorsal arcuate fibers* (cuneocerebellar tract) from the accessory cuneate nucleus which lies lateral to the nucleus cuneatus in the medulla. The dorsal arcuate fibers furnish the cerebellar connections of proprioceptive fibers (areas C1 to T5) which have ascended in the posterior funiculi of the cord.

The *middle cerebellar peduncle* (brachium pontis) consists entirely of crossed fibers from the pontile nuclei in the gray substance in the basal part of the pons.  *$ — ant. Spinocereb.*

The *superior cerebellar peduncle* (brachium conjunctivum) is the main efferent connection of the cerebellum. The *dentatorubrothalamic tract* arises from the dentate and other roof nuclei and is distributed chiefly to the red nucleus, thalamus and reticular formation. The fastigiobulbar tract also runs with the peduncle for a short distance before it enters the inferior cerebellar peduncle. As it leaves the cerebellum, the peduncle is joined by the only afferent tract—*anterior spinocerebellar tract.*

## The Synergistic Function of the Cerebellum

The cerebellum is responsible for muscle synergy throughout the body. It coordinates the action of muscle groups, and times their contractions, so that movements are performed smoothly and accurately. Voluntary movements can proceed without assistance from the cerebellum, but such movements are clumsy and disorganized. Lack of motor skill as a result of cerebellar dysfunction is called *asynergia* or *cerebellar ataxia.*

Although the cerebellum receives large numbers of afferent fibers, conscious perception does not occur in the cerebellum; nor do its efferent fibers give rise to conscious sensations elsewhere in the brain.

## Afferent and Efferent Pathways of the Cerebellum

The cortex of the cerebellum is furnished with an immediate account of the progress of voluntary motor activity by signals from many sources: First, it is informed of the commands being issued from the motor cortex and the pyramidal system by a simultaneous outflow of nerve impulses in the *cortico-ponto-cerebellar pathway*. This is a crossed path connecting one cerebral hemisphere with the posterior lobe of the cerebellum on the opposite side by way of the corticopontile tract and the middle cerebellar peduncle (Fig. 29). Further communication received by the cerebellar cortex consists of instantaneous reports which are sent back from the muscles through the spinocerebellar tracts. All sensory modalities, includ-

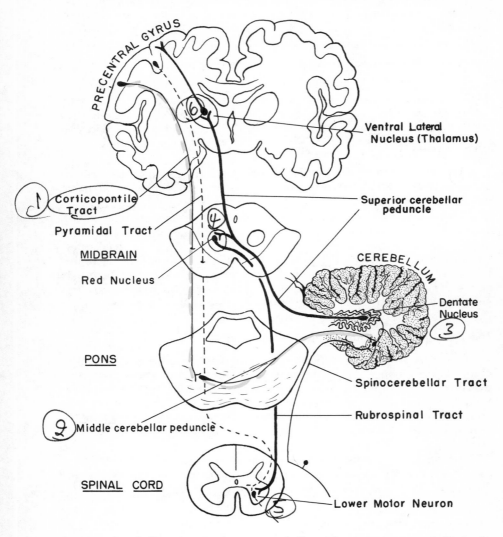

Fig. 29. Cerebellar circuits. The spinocerebellar and cortico-ponto-cerebellar pathways to the cerebellum are represented by thin fibers. Thicker fibers show efferent paths from the dentate nucleus to the spinal cord and to the precentral gyrus. The pyramidal tract is shown as a dotted line.

ing tactile, auditory and visual stimula, feed impulses to the cerebellum. These messages enter a vast pool of cortical neurons where, by unknown mechanisms, rapid correlations and integrations must take place.

After an evaluation of the afferent signals, the cerebellum is able to make an appropriate correction for any mistakes or inaccuracies of muscle activity. Nerve impulses are dispatched from the dentate nucleus through the fibers of the superior cerebellar peduncle. There are several routes over which these impulses may travel to reach the voluntary motor system and modify muscular movements. The first of these is the *dentato-rubrospinal path* leading directly to lower motor neurons of the spinal cord. Fibers from the dentate nucleus synapse with cells of the red nucleus which give rise to axons of the rubrospinal tract. This path crosses twice—once in the decussation of the superior cerebellar peduncle, and again in the rubrospinal tract near its origin—so that the origin and terminus are on the same side of the body. Another route traveled by efferent cerebellar impulses is the *dentato-thalamo-cortical path*. Crossed fibers of the superior cerebellar peduncle which by-pass the red nucleus ascend to the ventral lateral nucleus of the thalamus. Thalamocortical fibers from this nucleus relay impulses to the motor area of the frontal lobe. It is clear that the cerebellum influences the activity of the pyramidal system through these circuits. Impulses to both facilitatory and inhibitory reticular nuclei are transmitted by the reticulospinal tracts to the motor neurons.

## Feed-Back Circuits Through the Cerebellum

The general scheme of operation of the cerebellum allows nerve impulses to be returned, or fed back, to the same region from which they originated. In this respect cerebellar circuits are analogous to modern automatic control devices, or servomechanisms. The guided missile, for example, transmits radar signals which are picked up and fed to a mechanical computer. The computer, which may be thought of as analogous to the cortex of the cerebellum, detects any error in the missile's track and returns the proper radio messages to adjust its controls and put it back on course.

Briefly, the following are important feed-back circuits involving the cerebellum:

1. The cortico-ponto-cerebellar circuit has just been described and is outlined in Figure 29.

2. The vestibular-cerebellar circuit involves the connections from the vestibular nerve to the flocculonodular lobe, the fastigial nucleus, and fastigiobulbar tract to the vestibular and reticular nuclei in the brain stem.

3. The intracerebellar circuit involves the collateral fibers of the Purkinje cell axons that project back to additional Purkinje cells (producing the so-called "avalanche effect" of Cajal).

75

## Clinical Signs of Cerebellar Dysfunction

Disorders of the cerebellum, or of the fibers leading to and from the cerebellum, are accompanied by a number of characteristic signs, all of which concern the motor system:

1. *Ataxia.* Ataxia which is caused by cerebellar damage is manifested in several ways.

   A. *Disturbances of posture and gait* may be pronounced. Lesions of the midline region of the cerebellum cause difficulty in maintaining an upright stance. The loss of equilibrium is due to lack of muscle synergy and not to a defect in the pathway of conscious proprioception. Closing the eyes has very little worsening influence on this form of ataxia. The gait is staggering, not unlike that seen in drunkenness. A lesion located in one hemisphere of the cerebellum causes a tendency to fall toward the side of the lesion. If the patient attempts to walk in a straight line with the eyes closed, he may swerve to the side of the injured hemisphere.

   B. *Decomposition of movement.* An action which requires the co-operative movement of several joints is not properly coordinated, but is broken down into its component parts. For example, in bringing the hand to the mouth the joints of the shoulder, elbow and wrist may be moved separately and not grouped together in one synchronized movement.

   C. *Dysmetria* is shown by the inability to stop a movement at the desired point. In reaching the hand toward an object, the patient either overshoots the goal or stops before it is reached. When he is asked to point his finger directly to the finger of the examiner, the patient may instead point consistently to one side, a phenomenon known as *past-pointing.*

   D. *Dysdiadochokinesia,* or adiadochokinesia, is the inability to stop one movement and follow it immediately by the directly opposite action. This is apparent on attempting to make rapid alternating movements of pronation and supination of the hands, or by tapping quickly with the fingers.

   E. *Scanning speech* is due to asynergy of the muscles used in speaking. The spacing of sounds is irregular with pauses in the wrong places.

2. *Hypotonia.* The muscle tone is decreased which may be ascertained by palpation. The tendon reflexes are usually decreased on the side affected. A *pendular knee* jerk, in which the leg swings freely back and forth several times, is sometimes present.

3. *Asthenia.* The muscles which are affected by cerebellar lesions are weaker, and tire more easily than normal muscles.

4. *Tremor.* The tremor of cerebellar dysfunction is usually an intention tremor. It is evident during purposeful movements, but absent or

76

diminished with rest. Lesions which are most apt to produce tremor are those that involve the efferent pathways of the superior cerebellar peduncle. The movements are coarse and arrhythmic.

5. *Nystagmus*. The nystagmus which is frequently present with cerebellar lesions may be accounted for by irritation of vestibular fibers in the cerebellum; or it may be due to the effect of pressure on the vestibular nuclei of the brain stem ventral to the cerebellum.

Cerebellar defects are compensated for, to a considerable extent, by other mechanisms of the brain if sufficient time is given. Consequently symptoms are less severe in slowly progressing disease processes than in acute injuries of the cerebellum.

Somatotopical localization of separate body regions in the cerebellar cortex has been shown in experimental animals. It is important to note, however, that the right side of the body is under the influence of the right cerebellar hemisphere, and that any symptoms which occur unilaterally are found on the same side, as the lesion in the cerebellum. This contrasts strikingly with cerebral lesions which invariably produce contralateral effects.

## CHAPTER 15

# Lesions of the Brain Stem

Because of the compact arrangement of the structures of the brain stem, a single lesion nearly always damages several of them at once to produce a puzzling assortment of clinical signs. Logical interpretation of these effects depends on an understanding of the functional anatomy of fiber tracts and nuclei. The examples which follow illustrate some of the symptom complexes, or syndromes, associated with hemorrhages, vascular occlusions, tumors, or areas of degeneration in different parts of the brain stem. Many of these syndromes have been given eponyms, but since there is considerable lack of uniformity in their usage, only the more familiar ones will be named.

### Lesions of the Basal Part of the Medulla

Several of the individual cranial nerves pass close to the lateral side of the pyramidal tract before they emerge from the brain stem. A single lesion that includes the nerve and the tract at this point produces nerve paralysis on the side of the lesion and contralateral hemiplegia, a condition referred to as *alternating hemiplegia.* For example, a lesion of the right hypoglossal nerve and the right pyramid results in left hemiplegia combined with paralysis of the muscles of the right half of the tongue (Fig. 30, 1). The paralysis of the arm and leg is on the side opposite the lesion because the pyramidal tract subsequently crosses to the left. The usual signs of spasticity—increased muscle tonus, hyperreflexia, pathological reflexes and loss of superficial reflexes—will be present. The tongue deviates to the right side when protruded and, in time, the right half of the tongue will become atrophic.

An extension of this lesion across the midline may damage the left pyramid and produce additional signs of upper neuron involvement in the right extremities (Fig. 30, 1a). If the same lesion is enlarged in the dorsal direction, it will affect the right medial lemniscus and there will be defects in tactile discrimination, muscle, joint and vibratory sense (Fig. 30, 1b). Since the fibers of the medial lemniscus have been crossed previously in the lower part of the medulla, the sensory signs will appear on the left side of the body.

### Lesions of the Central Region of the Upper Medulla

A small lesion in the lateral part of the reticular formation of the upper medulla may include the nucleus ambiguus and the lateral spinothalamic tract simultaneously (Fig. 30, 2). When the lesion is on the

78

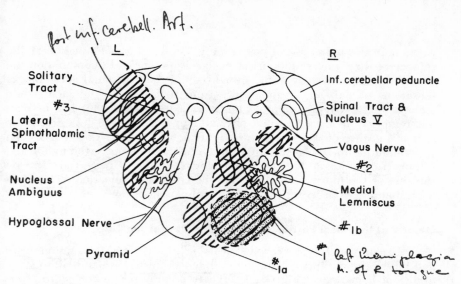

*post inf. cerebell. Art.*

L

Solitary
Tract

#3

Lateral
Spinothalamic
Tract

Nucleus
Ambiguus

Hypoglossal Nerve

Pyramid

R

Inf. cerebellar peduncle

Spinal Tract &
Nucleus V

Vagus Nerve

#2

Medial
Lemniscus

#1b

# 1 *left hemiplegia*
*1a*   *k. of R tongue*

Fig. 30.   Cross section of the upper region of the medulla. The cross-hatched areas indicate positions of lesions: 1. Alternating hypoglossal hemiplegia. 1a. Same with extension across the midline to the opposite pyramid. 1b. Same with extension dorsally to include the medial lemniscus. 2. Lesion of the nucleus ambiguus and the lateral spinothalamic tract. 3. Lesion of the restiform body, spinal root and nucleus of nerve V, vagus nerve, and lateral spinothalamic tract. Syndrome of the posterior inferior cerebellar artery.

right side, it causes loss of pain and temperature on the left side of the body, except for the face. The sensory effects are contralateral because fibers of the lateral spinothalamic tract are crossed near their origin. Destruction of the nucleus ambiguus paralyzes the voluntary muscles supplied by the right vagus and glossopharyngeal nerves. Failure of the right side of the soft palate to contract causes difficulty in swallowing and, on phonation, the palate and uvula are drawn to the non-paralyzed left side. Loss of function of the right vocal cord lends to hoarseness of the voice.

A larger lesion in this region may extend to the medial lemniscus and to the solitary tract. Interrupting the fibers of the lemniscus causes the additional loss of proprioception and tactile discriminative sense on the left. Destruction of the solitary tract results in anesthesia of the mucosa of the right side of the pharynx and loss of taste sense on the right side of the tongue.

## Lesions of the Dorsolateral Region of the Upper Medulla (Syndrome of the Posterior Inferior Cerebellar Artery)

The posterior inferior cerebellar artery, a branch of the vertebral artery, supplies the dorsolateral portion of the medulla. A lesion in this position is commonly the result of arterial occlusion by thrombosis. The damage involves the inferior cerebellar peduncle, the spinal tract and nucleus of the trigeminal nerve, the lateral spinothalamic tract, the nucleus ambiguus, the vestibular nuclei, and the emerging fibers of the vagus and glossopharyngeal nerves (Fig. 30, 3). Loss of function of the spinocerebellar tract results in cerebellar asynergia and hypotonia on the side of the lesion. Injury to the spinal tract of the trigeminal nerve blocks sensations of pain and temperature from that side of the face, while damage to the lateral spinothalamic tract is responsible for loss of pain and temperature sense in the limbs and trunk of the side opposite to the lesion. Because of its peculiar distribution, this sensory deficit has been called alternating analgesia. In addition to these features, the motor and sensory functions of the vagus and glossopharyngeal nerves are lost on the side of the injury, and there may be conjugate deviation of the eyes or nystagmus from irritation of the vestibular nuclei.

### Lesions of the Basal Portion of the Caudal Part of the Pons

A lesion which is so placed that it includes the right pyramidal tract and the emerging fibers of the right abducent nerve results in alternating abducent hemiplegia (Fig. 31, 1). There is an upper motor neuron type of paralysis of the left arm and leg as well as internal strabismus of the right eye. The tongue is usually not affected because the corticobulbar fibers to the hypoglossal nuclei run in the tegmentum and are not with the pyramidal tracts at this level.

Lesions of this part of the brain stem often extend far enough laterally to include fibers of the facial nerve, and will also produce a peripheral type of facial paralysis. When the facial nerve is included, the condition is sometimes called *Millard-Gubler's syndrome* (Fig. 31, 1a).

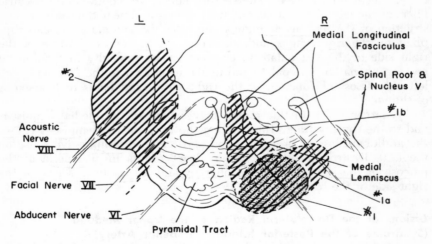

Fig. 31. Cross section of the caudal region of the pons. The cross-hatched areas indicate positions of lesions: 1. Alternating abducent hemiplegia. 1a. Same with extension laterally to include the facial nerve. 1b. Same with extension dorsally to include the medial lemniscus and the medial longitudinal fasciculus. 2. Lesion of the lateral area of the pons including the acoustic nerve, cerebellar peduncles, facial nerve, spinal root and nucleus of nerve V, and lateral spinothalamic tract. Pontocerebellar angle syndrome.

*Right side lesion*

A similar lesion with considerable dorsal expansion into the pontile tegmentum will involve the right medial lemniscus and the right medial longitudinal fasciculus (Fig. 31, 1b). The effect of interrupting fibers of the medial lemniscus is loss of position and vibratory sense on the left side of the body. The corticomesencephalic tract, which has descended from the motor eye center of the left frontal lobe, has already crossed and is contained in the right medial longitudinal fasciculus. Cutting the tract at this point abolishes the ability to turn the eyes voluntarily to the right—*paralysis of right lateral gaze*. The eyes may be drawn to the left by the pre-dominating influence of the non-paralyzed antagonistic muscles, but such an effect is temporary. The combination of symptoms produced by this lesion is known as the *syndrome of Foville.*

*1b*

## Lesions of the Pontocerebellar Angle

A slowly growing tumor which arises from Schwann cells in the sheath of the acoustic nerve close to the attachment of the nerve to the brain stem exerts pressure on the lateral region of the caudal part of the pons near the pontocerebellar angle (Fig. 31, 2). At first the symptoms are those of eighth nerve damage. There is progressive deafness, absence of normal labyrinthine responses and, sometimes, horizontal nystagmus. Later, cerebellar asynergia appears on the side of the lesion due to compression of the cerebellar peduncles. Damage to the spinal tract and nucleus of the fifth nerve abolishes the corneal reflex and causes diminished pain and temperature sensibility over the face on the side of the injury. A peripheral type of facial paralysis, also on the side of the lesion, results from the inclusion of fibers of the seventh nerve.

*2*

## Lesions of the Middle Region of the Pons

A single lesion in the basal part of the pons can affect the right pyramidal tract and the emerging fibers of the right trigeminal nerve to produce *alternating trigeminal hemiplegia* (Fig. 32, 1). There is spastic paralysis of the left arm and leg. The muscles of the right side of the jaw are paralyzed, and the chin deviates to the right. In addition, loss of the sensory fibers of the trigeminal nerve causes anesthesia of the right side of the face.

*1*

A lesion in the same region that extends deeper will enter the tegmentum of the pons and destroy the medial lemniscus. It also interrupts uncrossed fibers of the corticobulbar and corticomesencephalic tracts which have separated from the pyramidal tracts and, in this region, lie near the medial lemniscus (Fig. 32, la). In addition to left hemiplegia, there is now a paralysis of the left half of the tongue, the left side of the soft palate, and of the superficial muscles of the lower part of the left side of the face due to interruption of upper neuron fibers to the motor nuclei of the seventh, ninth, tenth, and twelfth cranial nerves. The lesion also destroys the corticomesencephalic tract before it crosses, and blocks impulses from the right frontal lobe which produce voluntary turning of

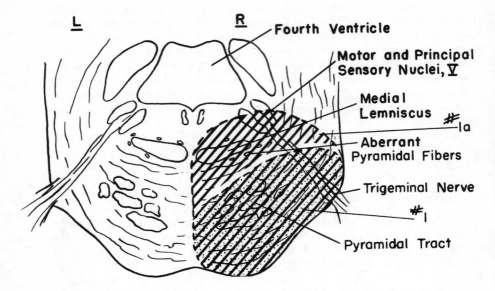

L          R   Fourth Ventricle

Motor and Principal
Sensory Nuclei, V

Medial
Lemniscus
#la

Aberrant
Pyramidal Fibers

Trigeminal Nerve
#I

Pyramidal Tract

Fig. 32. Cross section of the middle region of the pons. The cross-hatched areas indicate positions of lesions: 1. Alternating trigeminal hemiplegia. 2. Same with extension dorsally to include the medial lemniscus and aberrant pyramidal fibers.

the eyes to the left. This results in *paralysis* of *left lateral gaze*. Damage to the right medial lemniscus is responsible for loss of proprioception and discriminative touch sense on the left side of the body.

### Lesions of the Basal Part of the Midbrain (Weber's Syndrome)

A lesion of the right cerebral peduncle and the right oculomotor nerve produces spastic paralysis of the left arm and leg combined with external strabismus of the right eye and loss of the ability of raising the right upper eyelid. The right pupil is dilated by interruption of the parasympathetic fibers in the third nerve. The corticobulbar tract may not be affected, since its fibers diverge from the pyramidal tract at this level and shift to a more dorsal position as they continue downward. However, if the lesion extends dorsally into the region of the substantia nigra, it may include most of these fibers and cause weakness of the tongue, soft palate and face contralateral to the lesion. In this instance, the tongue will deviate to the left, the soft palate and uvula will be drawn to the right, and there will be weakness of the muscles of the lower part of the left side of the face (Fig. 33, 1).

### Lesions of the Tegmentum of the Midbrain (Benedikt's Syndrome)

A lesion of the tegmentum of the midbrain affects the fibers of the oculomotor nerve, the medial lemniscus, the red nucleus and fibers of the superior cerebellar peduncle (Fig. 33, 2). If the lesion is located on the left side, there is external strabismus and ptosis of the left eye from loss of the left oculomotor nerve. The right side of the body, including the face, shows a loss of tactile, muscle, joint, vibratory, pain and temperature sense from injury to the left medial lemniscus, which, at this level, has been joined on its lateral side by the spinothalamic tracts. Involvement of the red nucleus and the superior cerebellar peduncle, which contains efferent fibers from the right cerebellar hemisphere, produces tremor and irregular twitching movements of the right arm and leg.

## Lesions of the Superior Colliculi (Parinaud's Syndrome)

Injury to the superior colliculi (Fig. 33, 3) causes paralysis of upward gaze without affecting other eye movements. The anatomical basis for this is obscure, but experiments indicate that the area may contain a "center" for upward movement of the eyes. A pineal tumor could eventually cause this injury by pressure on the superior colliculi.

3

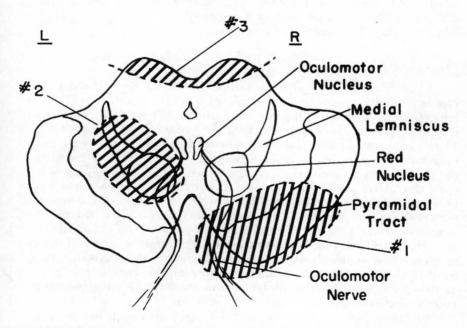

Fig. 33. Cross section of the upper region of the midbrain. The cross-hatched areas indicate positions of lesions: ·1. Alternating oculomotor hemiplegia (Weber's syndrome). 2. Lesion of the tegmentum including the medial lemniscus, the red nucleus, and fibers of the oculomotor nerve (Benedikt's syndrome). 3. Lesion of the tectum (Parinaud's syndrome).

## CHAPTER 16

# Vision

For vision to occur, reflected rays of light from an object must strike the eye, be refracted by the cornea and lens, and form an image on the retina. The optic principles are the same as those of any camera and the image that is formed is upside down (*inverted*) and turned left for right (*reversed*). The entire visual path within the brain is organized in a fashion which conforms with the peripheral optical system, so that the right hemisphere is presented with upside-down images of objects that lie to the left. This apparent distortion of position, however, is matched by other mechanisms of the brain. The motor areas of the frontal lobes, and the body-image contained in the somesthetic zones of the parietal lobe, are similarly inverted and reversed.

### The Visual Pathway

Light falling on the rods and cones of the retina, the first order neurons of the pathway, triggers a photochemical reaction in these cells. This initiates nerve impulses which are conducted to the cerebral cortex. The second neurons of the visual path are the bipolar cells within the retina. These cells synapse with ganglion cells of the retina whose axons converge toward the optic disc to form the *optic nerve* (N. II). Fibers from the macula, where visual acuity is sharpest, enter the temporal side of the optic disc. After perforating the scleral coat of the eye, the optic nerve fibers pass directly to the *optic chiasm* which is located in the anterior part of the sella turcica of the sphenoid bone immediately in front of the pituitary gland. A partial decussation takes place in the chiasm. Fibers from the nasal halves of each retina cross; those from the temporal halves of each retina approach the chiasm and leave it without crossing (Fig. 34). Optic fibers continue without any interruption behind the chiasm as two diverging optic tracts which go to the left and right geniculate bodies of the thalamus.

The fibers in front of the chiasm are designated as optic nerves, while those behind it are the *optic tracts.* Optic fibers terminate in the *lateral geniculate bodies,* superior colliculus, and pretectal area. Cells of the geniculate bodies give rise to fibers which form the *geniculo-calcarine tract (optic radiation)* to the cortex of the occipital lobes. The radiation fibers are directed downward and forward at first. Then they bend backward in a sharp loop and form a flat band which passes through the temporal lobe, external to the inferior horn of the lateral ventricle, and sweeps posteriorly to the occipital lobe. The area of cortex that receives

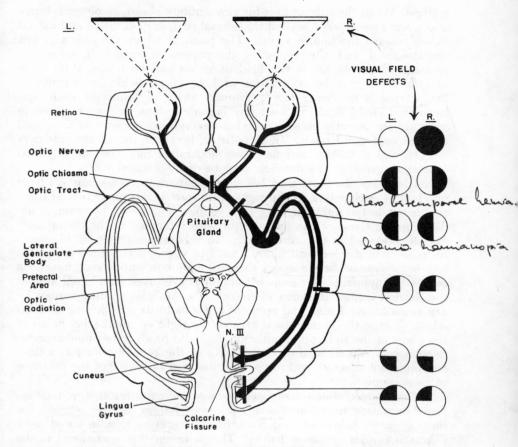

Fig. 34. The visual pathway. On the right are maps of the visual fields with areas of blindness darkened to show the effects of injuries in various locations.

the optic radiation surrounds the *calcarine fissure* on the medial side of the occipital lobe. The *visual area* (Brodmann's area 17) is also called the striate area because a cross section of the cortex contains a horizontal stripe (Gennari's line) which is visible to the naked eye. Areas 18 and 19, which adjoin area 17, are important regions for visual perception and for some visual reflexes, i. e. visual fixation.

## Effects of Lesions Interrupting the Visual Pathway

Destroying one optic nerve blinds the eye. Atrophy of the optic nerves affects some fibers but spares others, and instead of total blindness, there usually are areas of lost function in the peripheral part of the fields of vision of each eye.

The *visual fields* can be measured in detail with a perimeter, but a simpler way of examining them for gross defects is by the confrontation

method. While the subject fixes his gaze straight ahead, an object is intro-
duced from some point beyond the normal periphery of vision and moved
slowly toward the line of vision. The point at which the object is first
seen is noted, and after repeating the process in several directions, an
estimate of the extent of the field of vision can be made. With optic
atrophy there may be contraction of both visual fields, or a centrally
located patch of visual loss (scotoma) may be found in each eye.
Restricted visual fields, without any organic lesions, are encountered in
some psychoneurotic patients to whom everything appears as if viewed
through twin gun barrels. These patients, however, do not stumble over
objects, and if their visual fields are accurately measured on repeated
occasions, gross inconsistencies may be demonstrated.

A lesion of the optic tract behind the chiasm disconnects fibers from
one half of each retina. If the right optic tract is destroyed, visual function is lost in the right halves of both retinae. The result, however, is not
described in terms of the retinae, but with reference to the disturbance
that is produced in the visual fields. In this instance there is blindness
for objects in the left half of each field of vision, a condition known as
left homonymous hemianopia. Even though one optic tract has been
completely interrupted, vision is sometimes preserved in a small area at
the fixation center, the area of the macula. Macular sparing cannot be
explained anatomically, and opinions differ as to its significance. Lesions
which destroy the entire visual area of the right occipital lobe, or all of
the fibers of the right optic radiation, will also produce left homonymous
hemianopia. Visual acuity of the parts of the retinae whose functions
remain is not affected, and the patient may not be aware of the presence
of hemianopia.

The cuneus, which is the gyrus above the calcarine fissure, receives
visual impulses from the dorsal, or upper halves, of the retinae; the
lingual gyrus, below the calcarine fissure, receives impulses that arise
from the ventral, or lower halves. Thus a lesion that is confined to the
right lingual gyrus cuts off visual impulses from the lower part of the
right half of each retina. This produces a loss of vision in one quadrant,
rather than hemianopia. Since the images which are focused on the lower
part of the retina come from objects above the horizon line, there is, in
this instance, an upper left quadrant defect (Fig. 34). The visual impulses which go to the lingual gyrus travel in the ventral part of the
optic radiation. Consequently, a lesion of the ventral fibers of the right
optic radiation has the same effect as a lesion of the right lingual gyrus.

Lesions of the middle part of the optic chiasm are frequently produced by compression of these fibers from a tumor of the pituitary gland,
or a craniopharyngioma which lies near the midline immediately behind
the chiasm. The decussating fibers of the optic nerves are injured and
visual impulses from the nasal halves of each retina are blocked. As a
result, the left eye does not perceive images in the left half of its visual
field, and the right eye does not record images in the right half of its
field of vision. The defect is in the temporal field of each eye and is
therefore called *heteronomous bitemporal hemianopia*.

CHAPTER 17

# Optic Reflexes

## The Light Reflex

The constriction of the pupil which normally occurs when light is flashed into the eye constitutes the light reflex. The sensory receptors for this reflex are the rods and cones of the retina. The afferent pathway follows the course of the visual fibers of the optic nerve and tract as far as the lateral geniculate bodies, but instead of entering the geniculate body, the reflex fibers turn off in the direction of the superior colliculus (Fig. 34). They end in a region rostral to the superior colliculus known as the *pretectal area*. Internuncial nerve cells located in this region send axons around the cerebral aqueduct to the *accessory nucleus*, a rostral subdivision of the oculomotor nucleus. The efferent path begins with cells in the *accessory oculomotor nucleus* whose axons leave the midbrain in the oculomotor nerve and end in the *ciliary ganglion*. Postganglionic fibers coming from the ganglion enter the eyeball and supply the sphincter of the iris.

The response in the eye which is stimulated is the *direct reflex*. A *consensual light reflex* is shown by a similar, but weaker, constriction of the pupil of the other eye. The direct light reflex may be abolished by a lesion of the *optic nerve* or by disease which damages the retina severely. Lesions of the visual path which are located distal to the lateral geniculate bodies, however, do not interfere with the reflex fibers. In cortical blindness produced by a complete destruction of the primary visual areas of both occipital lobes, the light reflexes are preserved. The efferent path for the light reflex may be interrupted by damage to the oculomotor nucleus, oculomotor nerve, or the *ciliary ganglion*. Neither a direct nor a consensual light reflex is then obtained in the affected eye.

## Reflexes Associated with the Near-Point Reaction

When the eyes are directed to an object close at hand, three different reflex responses are brought into cooperative action.

1. *Convergence.* The medial recti muscles contract to move the eyes into alignment so that images in each eye focus on the same part of the retina. Otherwise the two images cannot be fused and *diplopia* will result.

2. *Accommodation.* The lenses are thickened as a result of tension by the ciliary muscles in order to maintain a sharply focused image.

87

3. *Pupillary Constriction.* The pupils are narrowed as an optical aid to regulate the depth of focus. The constriction does not depend on any change in illumination and is separate from the light reflex.

All three reactions may be initiated by voluntarily directing the gaze to a near object, but an involuntary (reflex) mechanism will accomplish the same results if an object is moved slowly toward the eyes. The *nucleus of Perlia,* a midline cluster of cells in the oculomotor group, is regarded as a center for convergence. Fibers probably go from the nucleus to both medial recti muscles. Other short fibers to the accessory oculomotor nucleus may bring about the associated responses of accommodation and pupillary constriction.

### The Argyll Robertson Pupil

One hundred years ago, Argyll Robertson described four cases of neurosyphilis in which the pupils failed to react to light but did constrict normally with accommodation. The sign later became a well-established clinical finding in syphilis of the central nervous system. Although the exact site of the lesions has never been proved, it is probably in the gray matter around the cerebral aqueduct. *Adie's pupil* is a benign condition characterized by a very weak light reflex which is delayed for several seconds and thus may be confused with the Argyll Robertson pupil.

### The Visual Fixation Reflex

Voluntary mechanisms turn the head and eyes toward an object which occupies one's attention and will bring the desired image into approximately the same position on each retina. The final adjustments, which are necessary to produce identical correspondence of the two visual fields, are carried out by the fixation reflex. If the object is moving, this reflex also serves to hold it in view, involuntarily following its progress by causing appropriate turning movements of both eyes. The afferent pathway of the fixation reflex is from the retina to the visual cortex. The exact location and course of the efferent path is disputed, but it is certain that it begins in the cortex of the occipital lobe and goes to the superior colliculus or pretectum. Fibers arising from cells in the tectum reach the motor nuclei of cranial nerves III, IV and VI by way of the medial longitudinal fasciculus. When the visual cortex receives images from the left and right retinae which do not match properly, impulses flow through the fibers of the occipitotectal tracts to bring the eyes into correct alignment for fixation.

The fixation is well demonstrated by a passenger who looks out of the window of a train at the passing scenery. His head and eyes turn slowly in the direction of apparent movement, then jump ahead quickly to fix the gaze on a new spot. This is done without awareness that the eyes are moving and is a true optokinetic reflex.

The fixation reflex is also used during the act of reading. Although we are unaware of it, the movement of the eyes along a line of print consists of several jerky movements (saccadic movements) with fixation pauses in between to allow visualization of a group of letters. These movements are not under voluntary control. Reading speed can be increased, however, by learning to take in more letters at once, or by making the pauses shorter. The difficulty of most slow readers does not lie in the oculomotor reflexes, but in the prolonged time required for each pause.

## Protective Reflexes

An object which is quickly thrust in front of the eyes without warning causes a blink. This reflex response cannot be inhibited voluntarily. Afferent impulses from the retinae go to the tectum of the upper midbrain directly. From here, impulses are sent in the tectobulbar tracts to the nuclei of the facial nerves which activate the orbicularis oculi muscles and close the lids. A very strong stimulus, such as a sudden blinding flash of light, produces more extensive activity in the tectal region which sends impulses over tectospinal fibers as well as the tectobulbar tract. Besides closure of the eyes, there will be a "startle" response of the whole body musculature and the arms may be thrown upward across the face.

## The Pain Reflex

Painful stimulation caused by pinching the skin, particularly at the neck, produces dilation of the pupils—the ciliospinal reflex. Although this reflex is well known, there are different versions of its pathway in the nervous system. Impulses which enter the spinal cord are said to stimulate sympathetic neurons whose axons ascend through the cervical sympathetic trunk to the dilator muscle fibers of the iris. On the other hand, it has been shown that the parasympathetic neurons of the accessory oculomotor nucleus, which constrict the iris, are inhibited during the response.

# CHAPTER 18

# The Autonomic Nervous System

The autonomic nervous system, though a part of the peripheral nervous system, is the functional division which innervates smooth and cardiac muscle and the glands of the body. It consists of motor (*general visceral efferent*) fibers only; sensory fibers (*general visceral afferent*) which accompany the motor fibers to the viscera are not a part of the autonomic system. The autonomic nervous system functions at the subconscious level and is integrated with other body activities. The hypothalamus exerts the primary integrative influence on the autonomic system. Descending impulses from the brain stem and cerebral cortex, as well as local reflex stimuli, may govern the activity of the autonomic nervous system.

The autonomic nervous system is a two neuron chain. The cell bodies and their fibers are classified as follows:

1. The *preganglionic neuron* is the primary neuron which is located in the brain stem or cord (intermediolateral gray column in thoracic cord).
2. The *postganglionic neuron* is the postsynaptic or secondary neuron which is located in outlying ganglia and innervates the end organ. The postganglionic neurons outnumber the preganglionic neurons in an approximate ratio of 30 to 1.

## Divisions of the Autonomic Nervous System

The peripheral autonomic nerves (preganglionic fibers) have their origin from three regions in the brain and cord which provides an anatomical basis for the two divisions of the autonomic nervous system. The *thoracolumbar outflow* consists of the fibers which arise in the *intermediolateral gray column* of the twelve thoracic and first lumbar segments of the spinal cord. This is the sympathetic system. The *cranial outflow* consists of fibers which arise in the accessory oculomotor nucleus, superior and inferior salivatory nuclei and the dorsal motor nucleus of the vagus nerve. The *sacral outflow* consists of fibers which arise from cell bodies in the intermediate gray matter of *sacral segments two through four*. These fibers form the pelvic splanchnic nerves (nervi erigens). The cranial and sacral outflow share many anatomical and functional features and together form the *parasympathetic system*.

The autonomic system also has a physiological basis of division. The terminals of the parasympathetic postganglionic fibers liberate acetylcholine and are classified as *cholinergic*. With certain exceptions, notably those fibers which terminate in sweat glands, *norepinephrine*-like sub-

Para — ACH — cholinergic
except. sweat gland — NE

*Sympathat. - adrenergic (NE)*

stances (sympathin) are released at the terminals of the sympathetic post-ganglionic fibers. The sympathetic system is classfied as *adrenergic*.

Many organs receive fibers from both the sympathetic and parasympathetic systems. When dual innervation occurs, the fibers usually have opposing effects (for example, parasympathetic fibers to the stomach increase peristalsis and relax the sphincters while the sympathetic fibers have the opposite effect).

*Stomach - para ↑ peristalsis ⎫ Symp*
*relax sphincter ⎭ opposit.*

## The Sympathetic Nervous System Division

The preganglionic fibers of the sympathetic system, which originate in the intermediolateral gray column, leave the spinal cord with the motor fibers of the ventral roots but soon separate from the spinal nerves to form the *white rami communicantes* which enter the *sympathetic trunks*. The latter are the paired ganglionated chains of nerve fibers which extend along either side of the vertebral column from the base of the skull to the coccyx. Some of the fibers of the white rami synapse with postganglionic neurons in the trunk ganglion (*paravertebral ganglion*) nearest their point of entrance. Other preganglionic fibers pass up or down the chain to end in paravertebral ganglia at higher or lower levels than the point of entrance.

Nonmyelinated, postganglionic fibers given off from the neurons in the sympathetic trunk ganglia form the *gray rami communicantes*. Each spinal nerve receives a gray ramus which is distributed to the blood vessels, arrector pili muscles and sweat glands of the body wall throughout its dermatome. The gray rami outnumber the white since they are given off from the ganglia of the cervical, lower lumbar and sacral segments of the sympathetic trunk which do not have white rami.

The *cervical part* of the sympathetic trunk consists of ascending preganglionic fibers from the first four or five thoracic segments of the spinal cord. Three ganglia are present—*superior cervical, middle cervical* and the *cervicothoracic* (stellate). The latter is formed by the fusion of the inferior cervical and first thoracic ganglia. In addition to providing gray rami for the cervical and upper thoracic spinal nerves, the cervical ganglia also give rise to *cardiac nerves* which enter the cardiac plexus to supply sympathetic innervation to the heart. The *carotid plexus* is derived from the superior cervical ganglion. This plexus follows the ramifications of the carotid arteries and furnishes the sympathetic innervation of the head. Some fibers end in blood vessels and sweat glands of the head and face; others supply the lacrimal and salivary glands. The eye receives sympathetic fibers which innervate the dilator muscles of the iris and the smooth muscle fibers of the eyelid.

The viscera of the abdominal and pelvic cavities are supplied by the splanchnic nerves. The *thoracic splanchnic nerves* (greater, lesser and least) carry the preganglionic fibers from the levels of ganglia T5 to T12 to the prevertebral ganglia of the abdomen. The latter ganglia include the *celiac, superior mesenteric* and *aorticorenal* which are located at the roots

91

of the arteries arising from the dorsal aorta. The *lumbar splanchnic nerves* carry the preganglionic fibers from the levels of the upper lumbar ganglia. The lumbar splanchnics terminate in the *inferior mesenteric* and *hypogastric ganglia*. The postganglionic fibers from the prevertebral (collateral) ganglia form extensive plexuses which follow the ramifications of the visceral arteries to reach the organs of the abdomen and pelvis.

Paralysis of the cervical portion of the sympathetic system produces *Horner's syndrome*. The pupil of the injured side is constricted because its dilator muscle is inactive. There is mild ptosis of the eyelid, but the lid can still be raised voluntarily. Absence of sweating and vasodilation on the affected side makes the skin of the face and neck appear reddened and it feels warmer and drier than the normal side. Horner's syndrome is commonly the result of a lesion of the cervicothoracic ganglion or of the cervical part of the sympathetic chain. It also occurs when a lesion of the spinal cord destroys the preganglionic neurons at their origin in the eighth cervical and first thoracic segments (ciliospinal center). Lesions which involve the reticular formation of the brain stem or the upper cervical segments of the spinal cord may interrupt descending sympathetic pathways from the brain and cause a Horner's syndrome on the same side as the lesion.

Since the superficial blood vessels of the head dilate after sympathetic interruption, the cervicothoracic ganglion is sometimes injected with a local anesthetic in an effort to produce dilation of cerebral vessels and improve circulation after cerebral thrombosis. It is difficult to evaluate the effectiveness of stellate ganglion block because many patients improve whether they receive the treatment or not.

Sympathetic fibers are known vasoconstrictors and operations have been devised to increase the circulation by interrupting this innervation (*sympathectomy*). Lumbar sympathectomy, which is performed to increase the circulation in the lower extremity, is the most common procedure.

### The Sympathetic Innervation of the Adrenal Gland

Stimulation of the sympathetic nervous system ordinarily produces generalized physiological responses rather than discrete localized effects. This is, in part, due to the wide dispersion of sympathetic fibers, but is augmented by the release of epinephrine from the adrenal glands which circulates in the blood and increases the effects of impulses in the postganglionic fibers. The medulla of the adrenal gland is supplied by preganglionic fibers (lesser and least splanchnic nerves) which end directly on the adrenal medullary cells without synapsing in an interposed ganglion. The cells themselves are derivatives of nerve tissue and, in effect, constitute a modified sympathetic ganglion. Pain, exposure to cold, and strong emotions such as rage and fear evoke sympathetic activity which mobilizes the body resources for violent action. Functions of the gastrointestinal tract are suspended and blood is shunted away from the splanchnic area. Heart rate and blood pressure are increased. The coronary arteries dilate. The bronchioles of the lung are increased in caliber. Contractions of the spleen release extra red cells to the blood. This activity was described by Cannon as the "fight or flight" phenomenon.

## The Parasympathetic Nervous System

The preganglionic fibers of the parasympathetic system are long and extend to the *terminal ganglia* located within (for example, the myenteric plexus) or very close to (for example, the ciliary ganglion) the organs which they supply. The postganglionic fibers, as a result, are very short.

The *cranial division* of the parasympathetic system supplies the ciliary muscle and sphincter muscle of the iris through the oculomotor nerve and ciliary ganglion. Secretory preganglionic fibers from the nervus intermedius of the VIIth cranial nerve synapse in the pterygopalatine and submandibular ganglia. Postganglionic fibers from the pterygopalatine ganglion innervate glands of the mucous membrane, nasal chamber and sinuses, palate and pharynx, and the lacrimal gland while the fibers of the submandibular ganglion supply the sublingual and submandibular glands. The otic ganglion, which receives preganglionic fibers of the IXth cranial nerve, supplies postganglionic fibers to the parotid gland. The vagus nerve supplies the preganglionic fibers to the heart, lungs, and abdominal viscera. The latter organs have the postganglionic neurons in associated plexuses adjacent to or within the walls of the viscus.

The sacral division, through the pelvic splanchnic nerves, supplies fibers to ganglia in the muscular coats of the urinary and reproductive tracts, colon (descending and sigmoid) and the rectum. In the pelvic region the parasympathetic system is primarily concerned with mechanisms for emptying. Under strong emotional circumstances these fibers may discharge along with a generalized sympathetic response and produce involuntary emptying of the bladder and rectum. The parasympathetic fibers are responsible for penile erection. Stimulation by sympathetic fibers and not parasympathetic, initiates the contractions of the ductus deferens and seminal vesicles to produce ejaculation.

## The Innervation of the Urinary Bladder

Motor control of the urinary bladder is primarily a parasympathetic function which, though purely reflex in infants, is brought under voluntary regulation in normal adults. The preganglionic fibers of the parasympathetic nerves to the bladder have their cell bodies in the intermediate region of the gray matter of sacral cord segments two, three and four. They enter the pelvic splanchnic nerves and terminate on ganglia which are located in the wall of the bladder (Fig. 35). Short postganglionic fibers go to the detrusor muscle and to the internal sphincter which guards the internal orifice of the urethra. Stimulation of the parasympathetic nerves of the bladder contracts the detrusor, relaxes the internal sphincter, and empties the bladder.

93

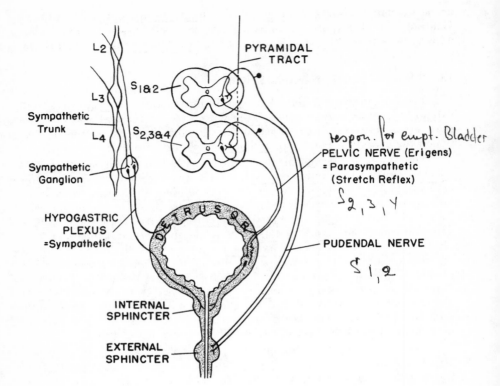

Fig. 35. Autonomic innervation of the urinary bladder. The postganglionic parasympathetic ganglion cells are located in the pelvic plexus and the bladder wall.

The *sympathetic* supply to the bladder originates in cells of the intermediolateral gray column of upper lumbar cord segments whose axons pass through the sympathetic trunk to reach the inferior mesenteric ganglion by the lumbar splanchnic nerves. Postganglionic fibers continue to the wall of the bladder and to the internal sphincter. The functions of the sympathetic nerves are uncertain. They may assist the filling of the bladder by relaxing the detrusor muscle and tightening the internal sphincter, but they have little influence on emptying mechanisms. Cutting the sympathetic nerves to the bladder does not seriously affect its function.

The external sphincter of the urethra is made up of striated muscle and innervated by regular motor fibers of the pudendal nerve along with other muscles of the perineum. The external sphincter may be closed voluntarily but relaxes by reflex action as soon as urine is released through the internal sphincter at the beginning of micturition.

The smooth muscle of the bladder responds to a stretch reflex operated by proprioceptors in its wall which send impulses to spinal cord segments sacral two, three and four. The efferent reflex fibers return impulses over the pelvic splanchnic nerves to maintain tonus in the detrusor muscle while the bladder is filling. In the uninhibited bladder of infancy, and in some cases of mental deficiency or diffuse brain damage, the bladder fills nearly to its normal capacity, then a stronger reflex response takes place and it empties automatically. Voluntary suppression of urination is dependent on fibers that descend in the pyramidal tracts from the cortex of the paracentral lobules of the cerebrum. It is generally believed that these fibers exert an inhibitory effect on the detrusor reflex. The sensation of increased bladder tension and the desire to void are conveyed by sensory impulses in the afferent fibers of the pelvic nerves and ascending tracts of the spinal cord.

Lesions of the dorsal roots of sacral nerves, or of the posterior funiculi, which interrupt afferent reflex fibers produce an atonic bladder. The bladder wall is flaccid; its capacity greatly increased. Sensations of fullness of the bladder are entirely lost. As the bladder becomes distended there is incontinence and dribbling. Voluntary emptying is still possible, but it is incomplete and some urine is left in the bladder.

Injuries of the spinal cord cause a derangement of the bladder reflexes which usually results in contraction of sphincter muscles and retention of urine. Following transection of the spinal cord in the thoracic region an automatic bladder is frequently established. After several weeks, reflexes in the sacral segments of the cord may recover and begin to function. The bladder fills and empties spontaneously, or after the skin over the lower extremities is stimulated by scratching.

## CHAPTER 19

# The Hypothalamus

## Diencephalon

The *diencephalon* is an ovid mass of gray matter situated deep in the brain rostral to the midbrain and ventral and caudal to the frontal lobes of the cerebrum. It is separated from the *basal ganglia* laterally by the fibers of the *internal capsule.* Ventrally, it extends from the *optic chiasma* to and including the *mammillary bodies.* The roof is formed by the *chorioid plexus of the third ventricle.* The rostral limit may be demarcated by a line between the *interventricular foramen* and the optic chiasma. The caudal extent is demarcated by a line from the *pineal body* to the mammillary bodies. Except for a small area of fusion, the *massa intermedia* or *interthalamic adhesion,* the two halves of the diencephalon are separated by the slit-like cavity of the *third ventricle.* The diencephalon is divided into the following regions: thalamus, hypothalamus, subthalamus and epithalamus.

## Hypothalamus  O T L M P

The *hypothalamus* forms the floor and a part of the ventrolateral walls of the third ventricle. The shallow *hypothalamic sulcus* on the lateral walls of the third ventricle demarcates the hypothalamus from the thalamus.

The hypothalamus includes a number of well-defined structures. The *optic chiasma* is located at the rostral portion of the hypothalamic floor. The *tuber cinereum* is the portion of the hypothalamic floor between the optic chiasma and mammillary bodies. The *infundibulum* (stalk of the pituitary) extends from the tuber cinereum to the pars nervosa of the hypophysis. The lumen of the third ventricle may evaginate into the infundibulum for a variable distance. The medial eminence is the portion of the hypothalamic floor between the optic chiasma and infundibulum. The *mammillary bodies* are paired, small, spherical masses located caudad to the tuber cinereum and rostral to the *posterior perforated substance.*

The hypothalamus may be subdivided into regions using the anatomical structures described as landmarks. The *supraoptic region* is the rostral area, the *mammillary region* is the caudal portion and the *tuberal region* is the intervening portion.

## Hypothalamic Nuclei

The hypothalamus consists of an admixture of neurons and fibers. The cells are somewhat aggregated and identified as nuclei. The more conspicuous nuclei will be identified in the three major regions. The following nuclei are found in the supraoptic region:

*Supraoptic nucleus:* straddles the lateral portions of the optic chiasma.

*Paraventricular nucleus:* is a group of cells dorsal to the supraoptic nucleus, in the lateral wall of the hypothalamus.

*Preoptic nucleus:* is the nuclear mass located between the supraoptic nucleus and the anterior commissure. Anatomically it is cerebral in location but it shows hypothalamic functional characteristics.

Several small nuclei are located in the tuberal region:

*Dorsomedial nucleus:* located in the dorsomedial portion of the lateral wall.

*Ventromedial nucleus:* located ventral to the dorsomedial nucleus.

*Arcuate nucleus:* located in floor of hypothalamus near infundibulum.

*Lateral nucleus:* located in floor of hypothalamus lateral to arcuate nucleus.

The following nuclei are located in the mammillary region:

*Mammillary nuclei:* are located within the mammillary bodies; usually subdivided into medial (larger) and lateral.

*Posterior nucleus:* located in the lateral wall of the hypothalamus dorsal to the mammillary nuclei.

## Fiber Connections of the Hypothalamus

The fiber pathways of the hypothalamus are numerous and complex. Connections are not only made with the cerebrum, brain stem and cord but intrahypothalamic fibers also exist. A few pathways will be described.

The following pathways are afferent:

*Olfactohypothalamic* (in medial forebrain bundle): The fibers arise in the medial olfactory area and some synapse in the preoptic and ventromedial nuclei. The olfactovisceral and olfactosomatic functions are served by these fibers.

*Corticomammillary* (fornix): The fibers arise in the hippocampus and terminate in the mammillary bodies and possibly preoptic nuclei.

*Stria terminales:* This is a small fiber, located in the terminal sulcus, which superficially demarcates the thalamus and caudate nucleus. The fibers extend from the amygdaloid nucleus to the preoptic and anterior hypothalamic nuclei.

Additional afferent fibers arise in the thalamus and globus pallidus (thalamo- and pallido-hypothalamic fibers). These are difficult to identify.

The following are some of the efferent pathways from the hypothalamus:

*Fasciculus mammillaris princeps:* is the conspicuous bundle of fibers originating in the mammillary nuclei. It bifurcates to form:

*Mammillothalamic fasciculus:* terminates in the anterior thalamic nucleus.

*Mammillotegmental fasciculus:* terminates in the dorsal tegmental and interpeduncular nuclei of the midbrain.

*Dorsal longitudinal fasciculus:* located in the periventricular gray matter of the brain stem. The fibers connect the hypothalamus with the reticular formation of the midbrain and thence parasympathetic nuclei.

*Hypothalamo-hypophyseal tracts* are the fibers which carry the neuro-secretory material to the pars nervosa of the pituitary. The fibers take their origin in the supraoptic and paraventricular nuclei.

*Medial forebrain bundle:* fibers from the hypothalamic nuclei join the bundle as it continues toward the reticular formation of the midbrain.

## Hypothalamus and Autonomic Nervous System

The hypothalamus has a regulatory influence on the autonomic nervous system. Stimulation of the *rostral portion* of the hypothalamus is excitatory to parasympathetic activity. It causes sweating, vasodilatation, and a decrease in the rate and force of the heart contraction. Lesions in this area allow sympathetic effects to have precedence which may result in increased cardiac activity, hyperthermia (fever) and panting. Stimulation of the *caudal portion* of the hypothalamus causes an excitation of the sympathetic system. The rate and force of the heart contractions are increased, vasoconstriction occurs, respiration is increased, dilatation of the pupil occurs and peristalsis is inhibited. One effect of a lesion in this area is the production of a hypothermic animal.

## Hypothalamic Pituitary Relationships

The tubules of the kidney are under the influence of an antidiuretic hormone (ADH) secreted by the pars nervosa of the hypophysis for the reabsorption of large amounts of water from the glomerular filtrate. *Diabetes insipidus,* caused by a deficiency in ADH, is characterized by an excessive urinary output (polyuria) accompanied by excessive thirst (polydipsia). The axons of the neurons located in the supraoptic and paraventricular nuclei carry neurosecretory droplets in the hypothalamo-hypophyseal tract to be released in the pars nervosa. The Herring bodies, seen in the pars nervosa, are believed to represent the stored secretion. It has not been determined whether the neurosecretion is the hormone or whether the polypeptide is modified by the cells of the pars nervosa. This region of the hypothalamus functions as an osmoreceptor and is sensitive to the salt content of the fluids which bathe the supraoptic and paraventricular nuclei. If the sodium chloride level is high, more neurosecretion is elaborated and released to facilitate additional water reabsorption by the kidney tubules. It is believed that the supraoptic nucleus is correlated with the release of ADH and the paraventricular nucleus is correlated with the hormone oxytocin.

There is also evidence that the hypothalamus influences the secretory activity of the pituitary pars distalis. No connecting fibers are present, but a vascular link is established by the *hypophyseal portal system* which is a network of venous capillaries which conveys the neurohumoral substance from the infundibular region and medial eminence to the pars distalis. The so-called releasing factor for ovulation has its origin in the medial eminence. The hypothalamus may also affect the secretion of the "trophic hormones" by the pars distalis. The precocious development of puberty which occurs in association with hypothalamic tumors may be the result of excessive gonadotrophin caused by an excess of neurosecretory material.

## Hypothalamic Centers and Appetite

The tuberal region has nuclei which are correlated with the feeding response. The *ventromedial nucleus* is designated as the "satiety center" while the *lateral nucleus* is the "feeding center." Small lesions in the ventromedial region of the hypothalamus cause experimental animals to eat voraciously. If permitted, they consume more food than they need and soon become fat. A lesion placed in the region of the lateral nucleus abolishes the appetite and leads to weight loss and emaciation. The Fröhlich or adiposogenital, syndrome is characterized by underdevelopment of the gonads and obesity. It has been associated with a lesion in the tuberal region of the hypothalamus.

## Regulation of Body Temperature

The anterior, or rostral, part of the hypothalamus plays an important role in temperature regulation by participating in mechanisms which dissipate excess body heat. When temperature of the blood rises, cells in this region send impulses over descending fibers to produce sweating and to cause dilation of the blood vessels of the skin which lowers the temperature. Cells located in the posterior part of the hypothalamus act to increase the heat of the body and prevent its loss. Fibers descending to the spinal cord constrict the vessels of the skin. At the same time sweating is inhibited and there may be shivering in which the somatic muscles generate heat.

Injury to the anterior part of the hypothalamus, as for example by surgery in that region, may impair the ability to dissipate heat and result in hyperthermia which is known as "neurogenic fever."

## The Hypothalamus and Emotion

It is clear that the hypothalamus dispatches the autonomic discharge of nerve impulses that produce the physical expression of emotion: acceleration of the heart rate, elevation of blood pressure, flushing (or pallor) of the skin, sweating, goosepimpling of the skin, dryness of the mouth, and disturbances of the gastrointestinal tract. However, emotional experience includes subjective aspects or "feelings" which are assumed to involve the cerebral cortex. Furthermore, mental processes in the cortex which possess strong emotional content are fully capable of bringing forth hypothalamic reactions. Pathways which connect the cerebral cortex and the hypothalamus are therefore considered to play an intimate part in the mechanisms of emotion.

Conduction pathways between the hypothalamus and the cortex are diverse and, in some instances, circuitous. They are concerned with the most primitive part of the forebrain, the rhinencephalon, which was formerly regarded as having primarily olfactory functions.

The major afferent connection of the hypothalamus is the *fornix*, a conspicuous tract ending in the *mammillary nuclei*. The fornix arises from the *hippocampus*, or horn of Ammon, which is formed by an infolding of the inferior surface of the temporal lobe along the line of the hippocampal fissure. Fibers of the fornix proceed backward on the ventricular surface of the hippocampus, then arch forward under the corpus callosum. The fornix completes its nearly ring-shaped course by turning downward and back to reach the mammillary body (Fig. 36). The efferent connection of the mammillary body is the *mammillothalamic tract*, a prominent bundle of fibers passing directly to the *anterior nucleus of the thalamus*. The anterior thalamic nucleus sends fibers to the *gyrus cinguli*, which is the long gyrus next to the corpus callosum on the medial aspect of

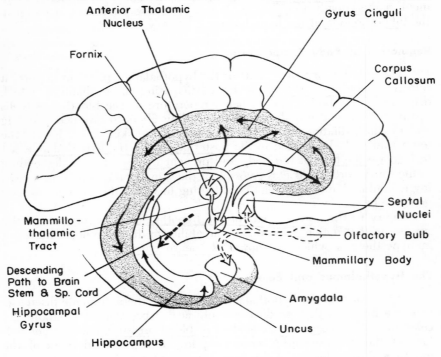

Fig. 36. Main connections between the hypothalamus and the cerebral cortex. The limbic lobe is shaded. Solid arrows show the hypothetical circulation of impulses during the experiencing of emotion. The thick dotted arrow indicates the descending path to the brain stem and spinal cord for expressing emotion. Olfactory afferent fibers are lightly dotted.

the cerebrum. The gyrus cinguli encircles the corpus callosum and, in its posterior part, is continuous through a narrowed strip (the isthmus) with the *parahippocampal gyrus,* the most medial convolution of the temporal lobe. Together the gyrus cinguli, isthmus, parahippocampal gyrus and the uncus, an eminence near the front of the hippocampal gyrus, form a ring of cortex known as the *limbic lobe* of the brain (Fig. 36).

It has been suggested by Papez that the hippocampus, fornix, mammillothalamic tract and anterior thalamic nucleus form part of a circuit by which impulses are transferred from the hypothalamus to the cortex and returned by the cortex to the hypothalamus. According to this theory, hypothalamic stimuli are projected to the gyrus cinguli by way of the anterior nucleus of the thalamus. Association fibers from the gyrus cinguli transmit this activity to other areas of the cortex and produce the emotional coloring of thought which is experienced subjectively during the expression of emotion. The reverse side of the circuit is offered to explain how emotional display is produced by psychic activity. Impulses are funneled through the cingulate gyrus and isthmus to the parahippocampal gyrus. Short fibers connect the parahippocampal gyrus with the hippocampus which lies beside it, but buried from sight. Fornix fibers to the mammillary bodies then carry the excitation to the hypothalamus which activates the peripheral autonomic nervous system. If this entire circuit is a reverberatory one, it may be possible for impulses to circulate continually and, by reinforcement, cause an emotional experience to be intensified.

Among the symptoms produced by the removal of both temporal lobes in humans is an attitude of indifference and a total loss of emotional responses. The operation removes a part of the hippocampus and interrupts the cortico-hypothalamic circuits. While this offers some tentative support, the Papez theory has, so far, remained largely speculative.

## CHAPTER 20

# The Thalamus

The thalamus comprises the dorsal portion of the diencephalon. The relation to the hypothalamus and subthalamus has been described previously. The thalamus is bounded medially by the wall of the third ventricle and laterally by the internal capsule. The dorsal surface of the thalamus has been covered by the overgrowth of the forebrain, and the roof of the thalamus is the chorioid plexus of the third ventricle. A groove, the *terminal sulcus*, which contains the *stria terminalis*, a longitudinal band of fibers, and the *vena terminalis*, demarcates the thalamus from the caudate nucleus along the dorsolateral margin.

The dorsal portion of the thalamus is subdivided into unequal thirds by the *internal medullary lamina*. This band of myelinated fibers demarcates the medial and lateral nuclear masses. The lamina bifurcates at its rostral extent to encompass the anterior nucleus. The centromedian nucleus is enclosed within the medullary lamina in the center of the thalamus. The ventral nuclei lie below the above lamina and adjacent nuclei and form the floor of the thalamus.

The thalamus serves as the station from which, after synaptic interruption, impulses of all types are relayed to the cerebral cortex. Processes of correlation and integration occur within the thalamus but conscious interpretation of peripheral sensory stimuli, except for the vague sense of their awareness, is not considered to occur at this level. The thalamus may be concerned with focusing the attention, perhaps by temporarily making certain cortical sensory areas especially receptive and others less receptive.

### Thalamic Nuclei and Their Connections

The thalamus contains a number of separate nuclei and, because of their complex anatomical relationships to one another, there is some disagreement concerning the subdivision, classification and nomenclature of these nuclei. A useful method for their classification utilizes their function and anatomical connections.

The *relay nuclei* are the ventral groups of thalamic cells which transmit ascending impulses to the cerebral cortex. The posterior lateral margin of the thalamus bears two pairs of small swellings, the geniculate bodies, on the lateral surfaces.

The *lateral geniculate bodies* (GL), in which the optic tracts terminate, relay the visual impulses to the visual cortex over the geniculocalcarine tracts.

The *medial geniculate bodies* (GM), which lie adjacent to the superior colliculi, relay the auditory impulses to the anterior transverse temporal gyrus via the auditory radiations.

PV    The *ventral posterior nucleus* (PV), which lies just anterior and rostral to the geniculate bodies, is the main sensory nucleus of the thalamus. The medial lemniscus, spinothalamic and the secondary trigeminal tracts synapse here. The sensory tracts from the face terminate in the medial portion of the nucleus (*ventroposterior medial nucleus*); while those from the remainder of the body are believed to enter the lateral portion (*ventroposterior lateral nucleus*).

The *ventral lateral nucleus* (LV) is the area within which the cerebellothalamic fibers carried by the superior cerebellar peduncle synapse. It also receives some fibers, via the thalamic fasciculus, from the globus pallidus.

The *ventral anterior nucleus* (AV) is the anterior division of the ventral nucleus. The studies on this nucleus are less complete though projections to the cerebral cortex (premotor area) have been proposed.

The projections of these nuclei to the cerebral cortex are shown in Figure 37.

The second functional group, the *association nuclei,* have a two way connection with the cerebral cortex but have no other specific ascending or descending connections. The interconnections within the thalamus are abundant, however. The cortical connections of the association nuclei are indicated in the non-stippled areas of Figure 37.

The *pulvinar* (PUL), the posterolateral projection of the thalamus, connects reciprocally with a large association area of the parietal, temporal and occipital cerebral cortex. It may be noted that this cortical region is practically surrounded by the visual, auditory and somesthetic areas of the cortex. Also the pulvinar is just dorsal to the two geniculate bodies and the ventral posterior nucleus. Thus, this complex may have a role in the association of visual, auditory and general sensory information.

The *lateral nucleus* (L), which is rostral to the pulvinar, is reciprocally connected with the portion of the parietal lobe posterior to the postcentral gyrus. It is frequently considered to consist of a rostral *lateral dorsal nucleus* (to region of precuneus) and a caudal *lateral posterior nucleus* (to superior parietal lobule).

The *dorsomedial nucleus* (medial) (M) is reciprocally connected with a large portion of the frontal lobe which is rostral to the premotor area.

The *anterior nucleus* (A) is located in the swollen anterior tubercle of the thalamus. This nucleus, in which the mammillothalamic tract terminates, has reciprocal connections with the gyrus cinguli. The latter gyrus is on the medial margin of the cerebral hemisphere, just above the corpus callosum, and is not shown in Figure 37.

The final functional group consists of the nuclei comprising the *diffuse conducting system.* The nuclei associated with this function are located in the internal lamina or on the extreme medial or lateral margins of the thalamus.

103

The *centro-median nucleus* is the most conspicuous nuclear mass enclosed within the internal medullary lamina of the thalamus.

The medial nuclei just under the ependyma of the third ventricle are known as the *midline nuclei.* Some of the latter may be located within the massa intermedia. These nuclei are more prevalent in the lower vertebrates and usually less prominent in man.

The *reticular nuclei* are the cellular groups which are located adjacent to the internal capsule.

The anterior nucleus, even though grouped with the association nuclei, also belongs to the diffuse projection system.

These nuclei are designated as diffuse projection because stimulation of any one of the aforementioned nuclei results in a widespread conduction of the impulse to the cerebral cortex with alerting and recruitment. These nuclei are considered to be the thalamic portion of the *ascending reticular activating system* by many workers. The diffuse conducting nuclei are not shown in Figure 37.

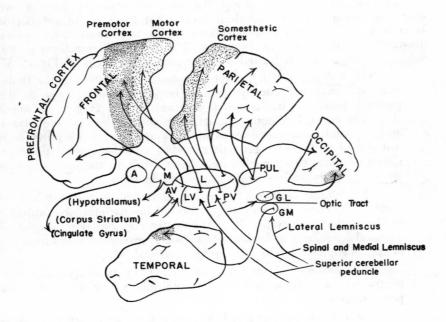

Fig. 37. Left lateral view of the brain with its lobes separated to show the thalamus and its principal cortical connections. The reciprocal corticothalamic connections are not shown.

| | | | |
|---|---|---|---|
| A: | Anterior nucleus | LV: | Ventral lateral nucleus |
| M: | Dorsomedial nucleus | PV: | Ventral posterior nucleus |
| L: | Lateral nucleus | GL: | Lateral geniculate |
| AV: | Ventral anterior nucleus | GM: | Medial geniculate |
| | PUL: | Pulvinar | |

104

## Epithalamus

The epithalamus is the most dorsal division of the diencephalon. It is the only roof portion of the diencephalon consisting of nervous tissue. The major structures of this region are the pineal body (epiphysis), the habenular nuclei and commissure and the posterior commissure.

The pineal body is the dorsal diverticulum of the diencephalon. It is a cone-shaped structure which projects backward over the tectum of the midbrain. Microscopically, it consists of glial cells (astrocytes) and parenchymal cells (pinealocytes). No neurons are present but there is an abundance of nerve fibers. Calcareous accumulations (corpora arenacea) are conspicuous features of the pineal body after middle age. The function of the epiphysis has been a controversial subject. At present, it is believed to have a secretory role which is associated with development and growth.

The habenular nuclei are located at the dorsal margin of the base of the pineal body. The afferent fibers to the habenula have their origin in the septal and olfactory nuclei and lateral hypothalamus and are carried in the *stria medullaris.* The stria medullaris forms a small ridge on the dorsomedial margin of the thalamus. The efferent fibers of the habenula, the *habenulopeduncular tract* or fasciculus retroflexus, is a conspicuous, dense bundle of fibers which terminates in the interpeduncular nucleus. Fibers from the latter nucleus descend to synapse in the motor nuclei of some cranial nerves. Hence the habenula appears to be a relay nucleus for olfactory impulses which regulate a primitive reflex (food getting).

The *habenular commissure* consists of stria medullaris fibers crossing over to the contralateral habenular nuclei. The *posterior commissure,* located ventral to the base of the pineal body, carries decussating fibers of the superior colliculi or tectum (visual reflex) and possibly fibers from other sources.

105

CHAPTER 21

# Rhinencephalon and Olfactory Reflexes

The rhinencephalon, which consists of the olfactory nerves, bulbs, tracts and striae, paraolfactory area (subcallosal region), anterior perforated substance and the prepyriform region, is relatively prominent in the brain of macrosmatic vertebrates. As vision is utilized more exclusively, dependence on the olfactory sense decreases. The vertebrates utilizing vision more exclusively are classified as microsmatic; the human being is an example.

### Peripheral Olfactory Apparatus

The peripheral olfactory receptors are found in specialized areas of the nasal mucosa designated as the *olfactory epithelium*. In man, the latter, generally pseudostratified columnar epithelium in type, is located on the superior concha, the roof of the nasal chamber and on the upper portion of the nasal septum. The receptor cells have elongated proximal processes which, grouped as filaments, pass through the fenestra of the cribriform plate as the olfactory nerve. The olfactory nerves pierce the surface of the olfactory bulb to synapse with neurons in the rostral portion.

### Olfactory Bulbs and Olfactory Striae

The olfactory bulbs rest on the cribriform plate. The so-called laminar architecture of the bulb is difficult to demonstrate in the human being. The rostral portion of the bulb contains three types of second order neurons:

Mitral cells are the larger, triangular cells which may synapse with a number of olfactory fila, tufted cells and/or granule cells. The synapses with the tufted and granular probably cause a summation of the olfactory stimulus.

Tufted cells are smaller cells and more peripheral than the above cells. They synapse with olfactory fila in a bushy-like synapse known as the olfactory glomerulus. The olfactory glomerulus also appears at the synapse of the olfactory fila with the mitral cells.

Granule cells are the smallest neurons of the bulb which serve either an association or summation function.

106

The anterior olfactory nucleus, in the caudal portion of the olfactory bulb, consists of a number of groups of neurons. These cells synapse with fibers of the granule or mitral cells and possibly further reinforce the olfactory impulse.

The paired olfactory tracts, which are narrowed caudal continuations of the olfactory bulbs, lie in the olfactory sulcus. The tract soon bifurcates into medial and lateral striae. Some of the fibers of the medial olfactory stria enter the subcallosal area and then the rostral portion of the anterior commissure to be returned to the opposite olfactory bulb for summation effect. The remainder of the fibers, which terminate in the olfactory trigone within the anterior perforated substance, are believed to be mitral cell processes.

The lateral stria, composed of mitral cell processes primarily, skirt the lateral margin of the anterior perforated substance to reach the prepyriform cortex in the region of the uncus. The primary olfactory cortex is considered to be the region in which the lateral olfactory stria terminate. Some fibers from this area are projected to area 28 (parahippocampal gyrus) which is known as the secondary cortical area. The olfactory system is the only sensory system which sends direct impulses to the cortex without the utilization of the thalamus as a relay center.

## Olfactory Reflexes

The olfactory reflex connections are numerous and sometimes complex. The following three pathways are described in their simplest form. The fact that reciprocal connections may be present is recognized but omitted for the sake of clarity.

Fibers arising, directly or indirectly, from the three terminal regions of the olfactory striae are conveyed caudally over the stria medullaris to synapse with neurons in the habenular nucleus. The latter nuclei are located at the base of the pineal body in the epithalamus. Fibers arising in the habenular nucleus, the habenulopeduncular tract, arch ventrally to terminate in the interpeduncular nucleus. Fibers extend from here to the reticular nuclei in the tegmentum which sends out fibers that are carried by the dorsal longitudinal fasciculus to brain stem nuclei (salivatorius superior and inferior and dorsal motor nucleus of the vagus).

The most primitive pathway involves fibers arising in the terminal areas of the olfactory cortex which are conveyed indirectly to the reticular formation via the medial forebrain bundle. Various cranial nerve nuclei may then synapse with fibers that originated in the reticular formation.

The following circuit probably enables one to determine whether an odor is pleasant or unpleasant. This pathway follows that of the limbic system which has been described previously. Fibers from the uncus extend to the secondary cortex in the parahippocampal gyrus. Association fibers connect the latter to the hippocampus and fibers from this area are carried over the fornix to the mammillary bodies. The fibers of the mammillothalamic tract* synapse in the anterior nucleus of the thalamus. Thalamic projections are conveyed to the cingulate gyrus which then sends association fibers into the cerebral cortex of the frontal lobes (see Fig. 38).

### Clinical Importance

Anosmia may be caused by a number of factors. The most common is the common cold. Other factors may be: nasal irritants, fracture of the ethmoid bone, certain drug intoxications, meningitis, psychoses and association with uncinate fits. Hyperosmia may occur in some hysterias and has been observed following drug addiction.

It also will be remembered that the subarachnoid space is in close approximation to the olfactory mucosa. This area is sometimes implicated in infections.

---

\* It will be recalled that the fasciculus mammillaris princeps, which arises in the mammillary bodies, splits into the mammillothalamic and the mammillotegmental tracts. The latter, as a consequence, could convey impulses to the tegmentum which could also stimulate motor nuclei.

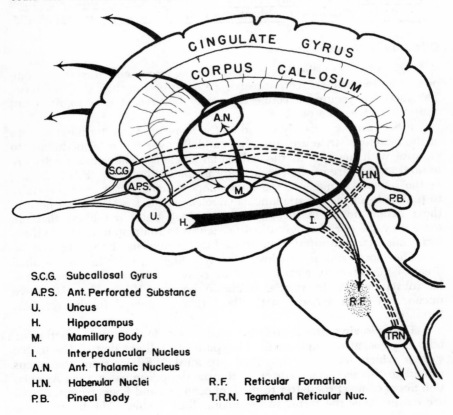

| S.C.G. | Subcallosal Gyrus | | |
| A.P.S. | Ant. Perforated Substance | | |
| U. | Uncus | | |
| H. | Hippocampus | | |
| M. | Mamillary Body | | |
| I. | Interpeduncular Nucleus | | |
| A.N. | Ant. Thalamic Nucleus | | |
| H.N. | Habenular Nuclei | R.F. | Reticular Formation |
| P.B. | Pineal Body | T.R.N. | Tegmental Reticular Nuc. |

Fig. 38.   Diagram indicating olfactory reflexes.

## CHAPTER 22

# The Cerebral Cortex

In popular opinion the cerebral cortex is thought of as the site of the mind and the intellect. Sherrington visualizes it dramatically as " . . . an enchanted loom where millions of flashing shuttles weave a dissolving pattern. . . ." Scientific thought considers it to be the area which carries out a final integration of neural mechanisms. These and other similar generalizations reveal the incompleteness of our true understanding of cortical mechanisms. The direct evidence that is available of the functions of the cerebral cortex in humans comes from three principal sources: (1) from the study of localized destructive lesions and surgical removals; (2) from the sensations and physical responses of conscious patients when electrical stimulation is deliberately applied to different points on the surface of cortex; and (3) from the patterns of response in epileptic seizures which arise from an irritative lesion in one part of the cortex.

## Neurons of the Cerebral Cortex

The convoluted surface of the cerebral hemispheres contains a mantle of gray matter, thickly studded with cells which are arranged indistinctly in six layers. From the surface the layers have been named: I. molecular; II. external granular; III. external pyramidal; IV. internal granular; V. internal pyramidal; and VI. fusiform. Besides the horizontal laminations, the cells of the cortex are loosely organized into vertical columns with radial fibers interspersed between them. Short axons make connections within the columns to form a great variety of closed chains, or loops. Some of the fibers which terminate on the cells of the cortex come from the thalamus (projection fibers); others arrive from widely dispersed areas of the cortex by way of long or short association fibers. The corpus callosum (commissural fibers) links together corresponding regions of the two hemispheres. The maze of connections present within the cortex offers innumerable opportunities for circulation of nerve impulses; the mechanisms which preserve orderliness instead of chaos in these circuits are unknown.

The pattern of distribution of cortical cells varies in different regions of the brain. The precentral gyrus, for example, does not contain granule cell layers II or IV. On the basis of such morphological characteristics— some obvious, others very subtle—several cytoarchitectural maps have been drawn up, parcelling the cerebrum into areas. Some areas have specialized functions, but for many no clear correspondence with function has been proved. The numbers by which Brodmann designated the anatomical areas in his chart, 52 in all, are still used frequently for descriptive purposes.

109

## Motor Functions of the Cerebral Cortex

The *motor strip* (area 4) from which willed movements are set into operation, occupies a small part of the frontal lobe rostral to the central sulcus. Massive discharges occurring simultaneously in all parts of the motor cortex are responsible for the tonic and clonic movements of an epileptic attack. Sometimes the conditions which tend to produce such convulsions can be recognized, but frequently no specific cause is discovered. A small focus of irritation near one part of the motor area is apt to precipitate Jacksonian motor seizures. These start as muscle twitches in one small, localized part of the body. As the cortical disturbance expands to adjacent parts of the motor area, the seizure spreads slowly to involve a whole extremity and sometimes one whole side of the body. Epileptic discharges in the vicinity of the frontal eye field (in area 8) produce contraversive seizures in which the eyes, and sometimes the head as well, are drawn to the opposite side.

The *premotor area* (area 6) lies immediately in front of the motor area and is connected with it by many short association fibers. This area is concerned with the development of motor skills and probably contains mechanisms for the elaboration of motor acts of more complex character than those represented in the motor area itself. The premotor area also has subcortical connections with the coordination nuclei of the thalamus (the ventral anterior and ventral lateral nuclei) by which it is linked to the corpus striatum and to the cerebellum. Since these structures have motor functions but are not a part of the pyramidal system, they belong to the extrapyramidal systems. The premotor area is the cortical extrapyramidal center.

In experimental animals, a lesion confined to the premotor area causes signs of spasticity, while a lesion of the motor cortex alone produces a flaccid paralysis. This suggests that the premotor cortex exerts a suppressor influence on stretch reflexes of the spinal cord. A narrow strip of cortex between the motor and premotor cortex has been designated as a specific suppressor strip (area 4s). Several other suppressor areas are claimed to exist. The suppressor pathways have not been demonstrated satisfactorily and much remains uncertain about the true nature of cortical suppressor mechanisms. Cerebral lesions in humans are usually extensive enough to include both the motor and premotor areas or their pathways simultaneously and the result is paralysis with spasticity.


## Frontal Association Areas

The large remaining part of the frontal lobe which lies rostral to the motor and premotor areas and the frontal eye field is known as the *frontal association area* or the prefrontal region. Besides its connections with the dorsomedial nucleus of the thalamus, this part of the cerebral cortex receives an abundance of long association fibers from all other lobes. It is believed that the frontal association areas are essential for abstract thinking, foresight, mature judgment, tactfulness and forbearance. These regions do not, however, seem to be primarily concerned with intelligence as it is customarily tested.

110

The *symptoms* of patients with general paresis, whose frontal cortex is undergoing atrophy from syphilis, are chiefly mental. There is usually a lack of a sense of responsibility in personal affairs, slovenliness in personal habits, vulgarity in speech, and clownish behavior, frequently accompanied by feelings of euphoria. Similar symptoms may be encountered with tumors of the frontal lobe.

The operation of *prefrontal leukotomy* consists of severing the connections of the prefrontal area with the dorsomedial nucleus of the thalamus by driving a pick through the roof of the orbit and sweeping it across the fibers in a coronal plane. Identical effects have been produced by passing a needle into the dorsomedial nucleus and destroying it by cautery. The resulting changes in personality include a loss of anxiety and mental agitation. The disturbed psychotic patient becomes complacent and agreeable. These benefits are not achieved without undesirable changes in character. The patient is easily distracted, lacks initiative, shows poor judgment and lowered ethical standards. The cortical scar that remains from the surgical lesion frequently causes epilepsy.

### Primary Sensory Receptive Areas

Three primary receptive areas of the cortex contain the terminations of specific sensory nuclei of the thalamus. Fibers from the lateral geniculate body conveying visual impulses go to the cortex of the lips of the *calcarine fissure* (area 17). A lesion here produces contralateral hemianopia. Fibers from the medial geniculate body carry auditory impulses to the *anterior transverse temporal gyrus*. Unilateral lesions of this area have little effect because both ears have remaining connections to the intact temporal lobe. The ventral posterior nucleus relays tactile and proprioceptive impulses to the *postcentral gyrus* (areas 3, 1 and 2). Sensations of touch, pressure and position are impaired on the opposite side of the body after lesions in this area, but pain and temperature sensations are not abolished. A receptive area for taste is probably present in the most ventral part of the postcentral gyrus.

The arrival of impulses at a receptive area produces well-defined sensations of light, touch or movement, but nothing is conveyed except raw sensory data. Here, an object is perceived as a meaningless pattern of light; a voice is heard as an unintelligible pattern of tone frequencies; and the touching of an object fails to disclose its shape. Before the arriving sensory messages are fully comprehended, they must undergo elaboration and analysis in an extensive cortical zone adjacent to the primary sensory area, the sensory psychic, or *sensory association area*.

### Sensory Association Areas

The *somesthetic* association area lies next to the postcentral gyrus in the parietal lobe; the *visual* association area surrounds the visual area on the medial and lateral aspects of the occipital lobe; and the *auditory* association area occupies a part of the superior temporal gyrus (area 22) near the auditory area. These association areas have the tasks of formu-

111

lating sensory stimuli into object images and of comprehending their meaning. This—the process of "knowing" or gnosis—must entail a comparison of present sensory phenomena with past experience. For example, the visual association areas must be called upon when an old friend is recognized in a crowd.

Lesions which are limited to the visual association areas (areas 18 and 19) do not cause blindness. Objects are clearly seen but they cannot be recognized and identified, a condition known as visual agnosia. Lesions of the parietal lobe (area 40) posterior to the somesthetic area produce tactile and proprioceptive agnosia. In addition to a loss of the ability to recognize familiar objects by feeling and handling them (astereognosis) there is frequently a disturbance of body-image. One extremity may be ignored, or there may seem to be a phantom third limb. Individual fingers may not be recognized and the left and right sides of the body may be confused.

The auditory and visual association zones border upon an extensive, and relatively "silent," area of the temporal lobe in which visual and auditory sensory experiences apparently are placed in storage as if they had been permanently recorded on sound film. It is here that the unknown mechanisms of memory, hallucinations and dreams may be located. By stimulating an isolated point of the superior temporal gyrus in a conscious patient, Penfield has been able to evoke a detailed and vivid remembrance of a specific, but unimportant, event which had taken place several years previously. Epileptic seizures caused by focal irritation in the temporal lobe may be ushered in by hallucinations of sound. Occasionally they are preceded by memory disturbances in which present and past experiences are confused so that an event of the present seems to be a repetition of something that has happened before, the déjà vu phenomenon. Memory recording is temporarily suspended during a temporal lobe seizure. The patient may continue to carry out purposive movements, but he remains amnesic for the attack. A further indication of the importance of the temporal lobes in memory function is that removal of both lobes in humans permanently abolishes memory of past experiences.

### Apraxia and Aphasia

Apraxia is loss of the ability to carry out purposive, skilled acts, even though the sensory and motor systems are intact. The accomplishment of a voluntary action requires a larger part of the cortex than the motor and motor coordination systems alone. There must first be an idea—a mental formulation of the plan. This formula must then be transferred by association fibers to the motor system where it can be executed. Generalized cortical damage may cause apraxia by interfering with the general planning of voluntary acts. Lesions in the region of the supramarginal gyrus apparently cause apraxia by cutting off impulses in association tracts. The idea is formed correctly but mistakes occur in translating it into performance. For example, when he is asked to drive a nail into a board, the patient may grasp the head of the hammer and strike the nail with the handle.

112

Facile use of language and speech is a remarkable attribute of the human brain—one that is shared by no other animal. A disturbance of language function as a result of brain injury concerns those forms of agnosia and apraxia which interfere with the use of written and spoken word symbols. This is known as *aphasia.* Beginning early in life, nearly every individual trains one hemisphere of the brain more intensively than the other in the processes of association. It is usually the left side of the brain that assumes the leading role and the person becomes right handed. With rare exception, language function is also relegated to the hemisphere of motor dominance. Aphasia does not appear unless a lesion is located in the dominant hemisphere. If it becomes necessary, the speech centers of the non-dominant hemisphere can be developed successfully in young, immature brains. Thus a right-handed child of five who suffers an injury in the left hemisphere will learn to speak perfectly again in a year or two. An adult may make this transfer but only after long intensive training, and even then the results may be imperfect.

*Broca's area* is located in the posterior part of the inferior frontal gyrus immediately rostral to the motor area for the tongue and larynx. A lesion of this area in the dominant hemisphere causes *expressive aphasia* (motor aphasia). Without any paralysis of the lips, tongue or vocal cords, the patient is unable to speak intelligibly. He knows what he intends to say, but cannot speak or the words come out in a garbled fashion. He has no difficulty in understanding others and recognizes his own errors. Penfield has found similar speech areas in the parietal and temporal lobes.

Lesions which involve the posterior part of the superior temporal gyrus, *Wernicke's area* (area 22), affect the auditory association cortex. In the dominant hemisphere this causes *auditory receptive aphasia* (sensory aphasia) and the patient cannot comprehend spoken language. Voices are heard and recognized, but the words seem meaningless. The patient can speak, but makes many mistakes unknowingly because his failure in comprehension includes those words spoken by himself as well as by others. Mixed forms of aphasia combining elements of expressive and receptive deficit are common.

*Amnesic aphasia* is the inability to recall specific names and is sometimes associated with lesions of the posterior part of the temporal lobe. Lesions which are restricted to the *angular gyrus* (area 39) surrounding the ascending tip of the superior temporal sulcus are said to produce a loss of the ability to comprehend the meaning of printed or written words and make reading impossible. This condition is known as *alexia.*

## The Internal Capsule

Afferent and efferent fibers of all parts of the cerebral cortex converge toward the brain stem forming the *corona radiata* deep in the medullary substance of the brain. When these fibers enter the diencephalon they become the *internal capsule*—a broad, compact band which separates the lenticular nucleus laterally from the caudate nucleus and thalamus medially. As seen in horizontal section, the internal capsule is shaped

113

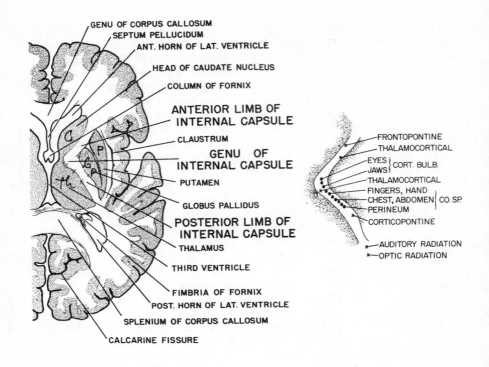

**Fig. 39.** Horizontal section of the internal capsule showing the relationship of various tracts within the anterior limb, genu, and posterior limb.

like an "L" with an *anterior* and a *posterior limb* joined at the *genu* (Fig. 39). Descending fibers of the pyramidal system are grouped closely at the genu and in the anterior two-thirds of the posterior limb. The corticomesencephalic and corticobulbar fibers for movements of the muscles of the head are located at the genu. Motor fibers of the upper extremity occupy the rostral part of the posterior limb and behind these are the lower extremity fibers. Fibers passing to and from the frontal lobe, other than pyramidal fibers, make up the anterior limb of the capsule, while those of the parietal lobe occupy the posterior part of the posterior limb. Optic and auditory radiation fibers are found in the sublenticular part of the internal capsule which is below the plane of section.

### The Cerebral Arteries

The *middle cerebral artery*, a terminal branch of the internal carotid, enters the depth of the lateral fissure and divides into cortical branches which spread in a radiating fashion to supply the insula, and the lateral surface of the frontal, parietal, occipital and temporal lobes. The lenticulostriate arteries are small branches, variable in position and arrangement, which come from the basal part of the middle cerebral artery to supply the internal capsule and other nearby structures. In the presence

114

of arteriosclerosis and high blood pressure one of the branches may rupture and cause hemorrhage into the substance of the internal capsule. The sudden collapse which such an accident produces is commonly spoken of as a "stroke." A relatively small hemorrhage in this region results in widespread paralysis because all pyramidal tract fibers are contained in one small area. There is usually complete hemiplegia with signs of spasticity appearing after the initial period of shock. Sensory losses may also be produced if the fibers to the parietal lobe are included. Extensive hemorrhages are fatal, but after a less severe insult, the patient survives and may regain partial use of his limbs through restored function in some of the damaged nerve fibers.

An occlusion of the main trunk of the middle cerebral artery by the formation of a clot (thrombosis) produces paralysis of the opposite side of the body with preponderant effect in the face and upper extremity, hypesthesia in the same regions, partial hemianopia, and total aphasia (if located in the left hemisphere of a right-handed person). When individual cortical branches are occluded, the symptoms are limited to the loss of function in that particular region. For example, if the inferior frontal branch on the left is thrombosed, there is weakness of the lower part of the right face and tongue with motor aphasia.

The anterior cerebral artery turns medially to enter the median longitudinal cerebral fissure. On reaching the genu of the corpus callosum it curves dorsally and turns backward close to the body of the corpus callosum, supplying branches to the medial surface of the frontal and parietal lobes, and also to an adjoining strip of cortex along the top of the lateral surface of these lobes (Figs. 40 and 41). A small recurrent branch (medial striate), given off near the base of the artery, supplies the anterior limb and genu of the internal capsule. Thrombosis along the course of the anterior cerebral artery produces paresis and hypesthesia of the opposite lower extremity.

The basilar artery, a continuation of the fused vertebral arteries, bifurcates at the rostral border of the pons to form the posterior cerebral arteries. These arteries curve dorsally around the cerebral peduncles and send branches to the medial and inferior aspects of the temporal lobe, and to the occipital lobe (Fig. 40). A separate branch, the calcarine artery, supplies the visual cortex. A number of perforating branches are given off which supply the posterior and lateral parts of the thalamus, and the subthalamus. Occlusion of the thalamic branches produces the thalamic syndrome. Sensations of touch, pain and temperature are distorted on the opposite side of the body. Superficial stimuli may produce disagreeable painful sensations, and agonizing, burning pain may occur spontaneously. In addition to the sensory changes, symptoms of cerebellar asynergia and tremor are produced in the extremities of the opposite side from damage to fibers of the superior cerebellar peduncle ascending to the ventral lateral nucleus of the thalamus. The calcarine branch of the posterior cerebral artery may be occluded independently of the thalamic branches. In this case the only sign produced will be contralateral hemianopia.

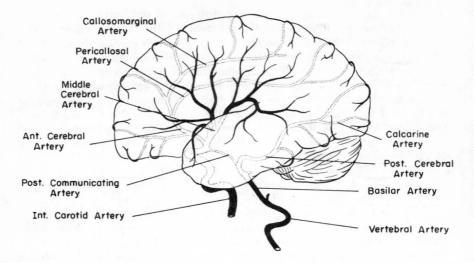

Fig. 40. Left lateral view of the principal arteries of the cerebrum. The anterior cerebral and the posterior cerebral arteries, on the medial surface, are seen as if projected through the substance of the brain.

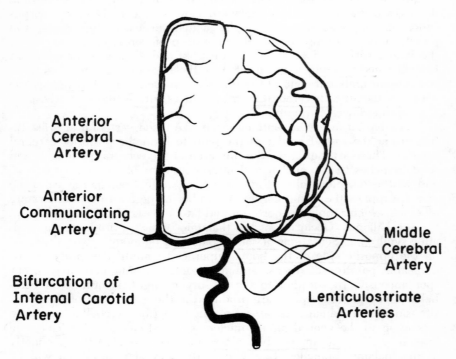

Fig. 41. Anterior view of the anterior and middle cerebral arteries of the left hemisphere.

## Circulus Arteriosus and Central Branches

The *circulus arteriosus* (circle of Willis) is formed by the junction of the basilar artery with the internal carotid arteries through the presence of a pair of posterior communicating arteries and an anterior communicating artery. (The communicating arteries are quite anomalous and the diagram purposely shows one posterior vessel somewhat smaller.) All of the major cerebral vessels have their origin from the arterial circle (Fig. 41).

The central arteries supply the structures within the interior of the brain—the diencephalon, corpus striatum and internal capsule. These vessels are branches of the arterial circle and may be conveniently considered in four groups:

*Anterior medial group*

Origin—anterior cerebral and anterior communicating arteries.

Distribution—anterior perforated substance to supply anterior hypothalamic region (preoptic and supraoptic regions).

*Posterior medial group*

Origin—posterior cerebral and posterior communicating arteries.

Distribution—posterior perforated substance.

Rostral group—tuber cinereum, stalk and hypophysis. Deeper branches penetrate thalamus.

Caudal group—mammillary bodies, subthalamus, and medial portions of thalamus and midbrain.

*Anterior lateral group*

Origin—primarily from the middle cerebral arteries; the *medial striate* or *anterior recurrent* from the anterior cerebral arteries.

Distribution—posterior perforated substance

Medial striate—anterior limb and genu of the internal capsule.

Lateral striate—basal ganglia and anterior limb of internal capsule. These vessels are also known as lenticulostriate arteries.

*Posterior lateral group*

Origin—posterior cerebral artery.

Distribution—caudal portion of thalamus (geniculate bodies, pulvinar and lateral nuclei).

*Anterior and posterior choroidal arteries*

These are considered to be central branches.

Anterior vessel arises from the middle cerebral arteries and supplies choroid plexus of lateral ventricles, hippocampus, some of the globus pallidus and posterior limb of internal capsule.

Posterior choroidal artery arises from the posterior cerebral arteries and supplies the choroid plexus of the third ventricle and the dorsal surface of the thalamus.

117

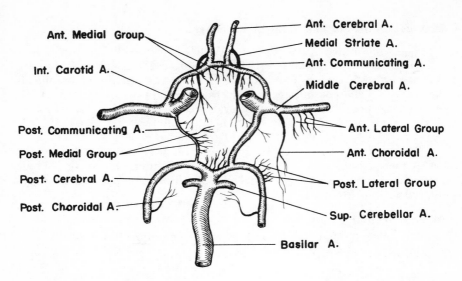

Ant. Medial Group

Int. Carotid A.

Post. Communicating A.

Post. Medial Group

Post. Cerebral A.

Post. Choroidal A.

Ant. Cerebral A.

Medial Striate A.

Ant. Communicating A.

Middle Cerebral A.

Ant. Lateral Group

Ant. Choroidal A.

Post. Lateral Group

Sup. Cerebellar A.

Basilar A.

Fig. 42.   Diagram illustrating the origin of the central branches from the circulus arteriosus.

## Angiography

Angiography or arteriography refers to the procedure in which arteries of the brain (generally) are studied by x-ray following injection of the vessels with radiopaque material. The internal carotid or the vertebral arteries generally serve as the site of injection.

Cerebral angiography has been useful in determining the site of aneurysms and any anomalous development of the larger branches of the cerebral arterial circle. Edema or hemorrhage and tumors sometimes may be localized by the alteration in the arterial pattern.

Generally, the smaller terminal arteries are not identified by this procedure. Injection of the internal carotid artery outlines the anterior and middle cerebral arteries. The major branches of the basilar artery (cerebellars and posterior cerebral arteries) are outlined following injection of the vertebral artery. The posterior communicating artery, if it is sizable, might be apparent following either injection.

## CHAPTER 23

# The Corpus Striatum
# and Subthalamus

The pyramidal system appears only in animals which possess a well-developed cerebral cortex. In other vertebrates, motor activity is controlled by the corpus striatum and the subthalamus. The movements performed by these more primitive animals are rapid and well coordinated, but they always have a more or less instinctive and stereotyped character. With the evolution of a larger cerebral cortex the old motor system becomes subordinate and secondary to the newly acquired pyramidal system. Most mammals, however, are still able to use the striatal system for habitual, or semi-automatic activities. The cat, for example, continues to walk without noticeable difficulty after the motor cortex has been removed. Humans are more dependent on the pyramidal system and suffer a more severe loss of motor function when it is damaged. But even in humans, certain involuntary movements may be demonstrated in paralyzed muscles—the so-called associated movements which occur habitually in accompaniment with normal voluntary motor acts.

### Non-Pyramidal or Extrapyramidal Motor Systems

To carry out motor acts properly the pyramidal system needs cooperation from three other sources: the vestibular system together with proprioception; the cerebellar system; and the corpus striatum. All of these are extrapyramidal in the true sense of the word, but ordinarily it is the striatal extrapyramidal system that is meant when the name "extrapyramidal" is used without further qualification.

The terms which are applied to the subcortical nuclei of the striatal extrapyramidal system are not altogether appropriate, and their usage is inconsistent. From the standpoint of traditional anatomy the corpus striatum consists of the caudate nucleus, the putamen, the globus pallidus and internal capsule; the basal ganglia include the caudate nucleus, the putamen, the globus pallidus, the amygdala and the claustrum. It is now recognized that the internal capsule, the amygdala and the claustrum do not belong to the extrapyramidal system. At times the globus pallidus is referred to as a separate division, the pallidum, while the caudate nucleus and the putamen are taken collectively as the corpus striatum. Others may include the substantia nigra and subthalamic nucleus with the basal ganglia. The term "basal ganglia" will be used here to refer to the main group of extrapyramidal nuclei: the caudate, putamen and globus pallidus.

119

## The Striatal Extrapyramidal System

The *caudate nucleus* occupies a position in the floor of the lateral ventricle, dorsolateral to the thalamus. The bulge at the cephalic end of the caudate is known as the *head.* The *body* passes backward at the side of the thalamus and tapers gradually to form the *tail* which curves ventrally and follows the inferior horn of the lateral ventricle into the temporal lobe ending near the amygdala.

The *lenticular,* or *lentiform nucleus* is a thumb-sized mass wedged against the lateral side of the internal capsule. It is separated from the caudate nucleus by fibers of the internal capsule except in the cephalic part where these two nuclear masses fuse around the border of the anterior limb of the capsule. The lenticular nucleus is divided into the *putamen* and the *globus pallidus.* The putamen is the lateral portion having the same histological appearance as the caudate nucleus. The globus pallidus, in the medial region of the lenticular nucleus, contains more large cells and is transversed by many myelinated fibers which accounts for its pale appearance in the fresh state.

The *subthalamus*—closely related to the corpus striatum in functions —contains the *zona incerta* (located between the fasciculus lenticularis and the thalamic fasciculus), the *subthalamic reticular nucleus* and the *subthalamic nucleus* (Luys). The zona incerta and the subthalamic reticular nucleus (the scattered cells in the prerubral field) are considered to be a rostral continuation of the midbrain reticular formation by some. The rostral portions of the substantia nigra and the red nucleus may extend into the region. The subthalamic nucleus, lens-shaped and lying along the medial border of the internal capsule, is contiguous to the substantia nigra at its caudal extent. The main afferent fibers are received from the globus pallidus over the fasciculus lenticularis. The main efferent fibers are projected to the globus pallidus (not shown in Fig. 43).

## Connections of the Corpus Striatum

The entire outflow of *efferent* fibers from the corpus striatum probably comes from the globus pallidus. Some of these fibers stream directly through the internal capsule and, on reaching the medial side, form a bundle which is known as the *fasciculus lenticularis* (Forel's field H₂). Other fibers from the globus pallidus sweep around the medial border of the internal capsule to form a loop, the *ansa lenticularis* (Fig. 43). Both sets of fibers enter the region of the subthalamus where some terminals are given off to the subthalamic nucleus. Many fibers continue through the subthalamic region and turn dorsally to reach the ventral anterior and ventral lateral nuclei of the *thalamus.* These ascending fibers are closely applied to the ventral surface of the thalamus and are known as the *fasciculus thalamicus* (Forel's field H₁). Some pallidal fibers also descend from the subthalamus to enter an area of diffusely arranged cells and fibers rostral to the red nucleus which is called the *prerubral field* (Forel's field H).

Afferent connections to the corpus striatum are not conspicuous and the details of their arrangement are not thoroughly established. It is certain that the caudate nucleus sends most of its fibers to the putamen and

120

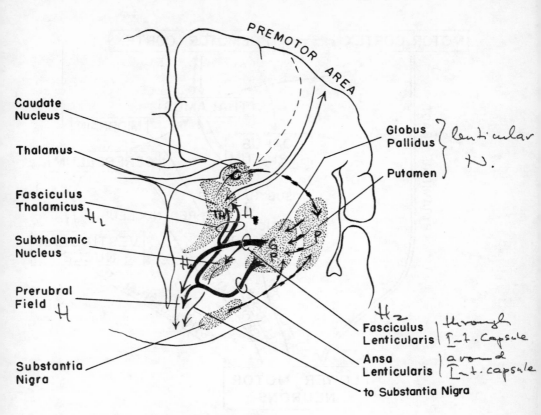

Fig. 43. Chief connections of the corpus striatum and the subthalamus.

that the putamen, in turn, sends an abundance of short fibers to the globus pallidus. The putamen and the globus pallidus receive some fibers from the substantia nigra. The thalamus (centrum medianum, primarily) sends fibers to the caudate nucleus and the putamen. Connections from the premotor cortex to the caudate and putamen have been demonstrated in some mammals. These projections have been found to be topically oriented in the anteroposterior and mediolateral dimensions.

Considering the large size and importance of the corpus striatum, surprisingly little is known of how it operates in normal motor performance. The caudate nucleus and the putamen are presumed to "tone down" or inhibit the activity of the globus pallidus. The globus pallidus itself is thought to be a mechanism for motor facilitation acting in two directions: (1) on the premotor and motor cortex through the thalamic fasciculus and the cortical projections of the ventral anterior and ventral lateral nuclei; and (2) on lower neurons of the spinal cord by way of the subthalamus, the prerubral field, the reticular formation of the midbrain and reticulospinal tracts. The left corpus striatum exerts its influence on the right side of the body. Fig. 44 shows, in schematic form, the connections of the striatal extrapyramidal system in relation to other extrapyramidal systems.

121

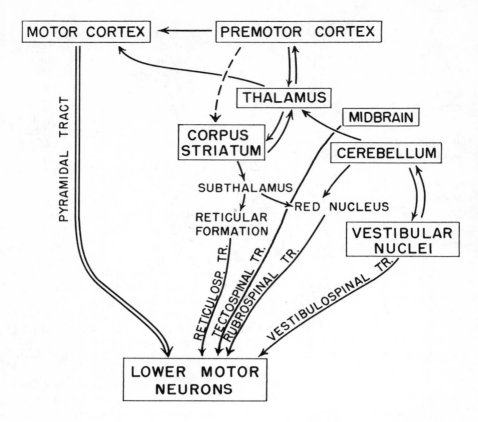

Fig. 44. Schematic diagram of the pyramidal and extrapyramidal systems.

### Extrapyramidal Motor Disorders

*Parkinson's disease*, or paralysis agitans, is a common disease associated with degeneration in various parts of the basal ganglia and in the substantia nigra. The deep reflexes are usually normal, but muscle tonus is increased in a manner described as rigidity. By passively flexing or extending one of the extremities an increased resistance is felt which gives way and returns in an alternating, jerky fashion like a cog-wheel. The rigidity of Parkinsonism affects all muscles without the special emphasis on the flexors of the upper extremity and the extensors of the lower extremity seen in disease of the pyramidal system. In addition there is tremor which is likely to be worse in a position of relaxation than when a voluntary movement is being carried out (resting tremor). Alternating movements of flexing and extending the fingers produce a characteristic "pill-rolling" tremor. The lines of the face are smooth, the expression fixed (masked face), and there is no spontaneous emotional response. The patient stands with head and shoulders stooped and walks with short, shuffling steps. The arms are held at the sides and do not

122

swing in rhythm with the legs as they should, automatically. Although there is difficulty in starting to take the first steps, once under way the pace becomes more and more rapid, and the patient has trouble in stopping his progress when he reaches his goal. Parkinsonism patients show degenerate changes in the pallidum and substantia nigra (loss of and degeneration of neurons and an increase of glial cells). Destruction of the globus pallidus or the ansa lenticularis will stop the tremor on the opposite side of the body, and various surgical procedures to accomplish this aim have been attempted.

Chorea is also caused by damage to the basal ganglia, but instead of rigidity the chief manifestations are sudden, involuntary muscle movements. Choreiform movements are quick, jerky and purposeless. Facial grimaces may occur, or any part of the body may be affected. A vascular lesion in the basal ganglia may produce hemichorea involving only one side of the body. *Sydenham's chorea* occurs in children as a complication of rheumatic fever, but the damage is not permanent and recovery is complete. *Huntington's chorea* is an inherited disease with defects in the cerebral cortex as well as in the corpus striatum. This disease becomes progressively worse and leads to severe mental deterioration.

Athetosis is a form of striatal disease in which slow, writhing movements of a worm-like character appear in the extremities, chiefly in the fingers and wrists. Athetosis is frequently seen in association with spastic paralysis of the extremities in infants with brain damage which occurred at, or prior to birth.

Hemiballismus is an uncommon disease which is characterized by continued wild, flail-like movements of one arm. This is caused by a small lesion which damages the subthalamic nucleus on the opposite side.

## CHAPTER 24

# The Cerebrospinal Fluid

The brain and spinal cord are suspended in cerebrospinal fluid, a clear watery liquid which fills the subarachnoid space surrounding them. The four ventricles of the brain are also filled with this fluid. The total quantity of fluid in adults is estimated to be 135 cc. on the average. It is constantly being renewed by the production and reabsorption of some 400 to 500 cc. of cerebrospinal fluid daily, a rate sufficient to replace it three times in twenty-four hours. Small amounts of protein, sugar, chlorides, and a very few lymphocytes (3 to 5 per cu. mm.) are present in the fluid. Its general composition is that of a blood ultrafiltrate passed through a semipermeable membrane with some modifications due to selective action.

### Formation and Circulation of Cerebrospinal Fluid

Most of the fluid is formed in the choroid plexuses which are tufts of dilated capillaries that project into the walls of the ventricles in certain regions. There are two large plexuses in the floor of the lateral ventricles supplemented by smaller ones in the roofs of the third and fourth ventricles.

There is slow movement of fluid from the ventricles into the subarachnoid spaces from which it is absorbed by cerebral veins and removed by the blood stream. The fluid leaves the lateral ventricles through the *interventricular foramina,* traverses the third ventricle, and reaches the fourth ventricle by way of the *cerebral aqueduct*—the narrowest passageway of its entire route (Fig. 45). Three openings in the fourth ventricle allow the cerebrospinal fluid to pass from the internal channels into the subarachnoid space outside the brain. The two *lateral ventricular* apertures are located in the lateral recesses of the fourth ventricle; the *median ventricular aperture* is in the midline of the roof of the fourth ventricle. Small pockets of cerebrospinal fluid are found within the subarachnoid space in various locations around the base of the brain. The largest of these is the *cisterna magna* between the inferior surface of the cerebellum and the medulla. Other cisterns, the pontine, interpeduncular and chiasmatic, lie between the base of the brain and the floor of the cranial cavity. The *cisterna superior* (*cisterna ambiens*) is the pocket of fluid which lies dorsal to the midbrain.

Spinal fluid fills the tubular extension of the subarachnoid space which forms a sleeve around the spinal cord. The lower limit of this space is variable, but on the average it is at the body of the second sacral vertebra, considerably below the end of the spinal cord. Although the spinal

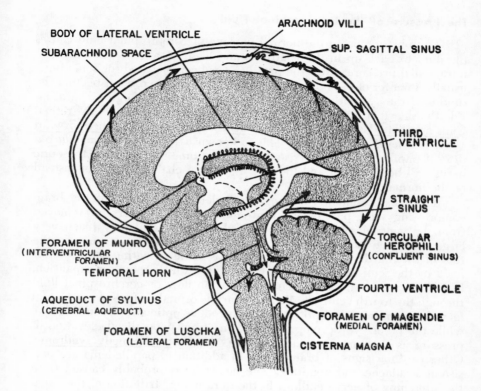

Fig. 45.   The circulation of the cerebrospinal fluid.

subarachnoid space is, in effect, a blind pocket, exchange of spinal fluid takes place by a slow mixing process induced by changes in posture.

Cerebrospinal fluid diffuses upward from the basal areas of the brain over the convexities of the hemispheres until it reaches the *arachnoid villi* in the walls of the superior sagittal sinus. It is absorbed from these villi and incorporated into the venous blood stream. Supplementary routes for reabsorption of cerebrospinal fluid have been proposed, but it is questionable whether these are very effective. A small amount may be absorbed from the spinal space by the vessels of the sheaths of emerging nerves. The veins and capillaries of the pia mater may also be capable of removing some cerebrospinal fluid.

The *Virchow-Robin* spaces are funnel-like extensions from the subarachnoid space which surround the walls of blood vessels as they enter the substance of the brain. For many years it was believed that these perivascular spaces were filled with cerebrospinal fluid and that they continued around the capillaries to connect with small fluid spaces around neurons. On the basis of studies made with the electron microscope it has been concluded that the Virchow-Robin spaces do not extend beyond arterioles.

## The Pressure of the Cerebrospinal Fluid

Any obstruction to the normal passage of cerebrospinal fluid causes the fluid to back up in the ventricles and leads to a general increase of intracranial pressure. After the pressure has been elevated for some time, usually a matter of days or weeks, the effect can be seen by inspecting the fundus of the eye with an ophthalmoscope. Due to the high pressure inside the sleeve of dura mater which surrounds the optic nerve, the retinal veins are dilated and the optic nerve head (optic disc) is pushed forward above the level of the retina. This is known as *papilledema*, or *choked disc*. If papilledema has persisted for a long time, the fibers of the optic nerve will be damaged and the disc assumes a chalk-white color instead of the normal pale pink.

The most common cause of papilledema is a tumor of the brain compressing some part of the ventricular system. Tumors far removed from the ventricles may not produce obstruction until they reach very large size. A tumor of the cerebellum generally exerts pressure on the roof of the fourth ventricle, and, since it is confined within the posterior fossa by the semi-rigid tentorium cerebelli with little room for expansion, it is likely to cause early obstruction to the flow of cerebrospinal fluid through the fourth ventricle. Tumors near the orbital surface of one frontal lobe may compress the optic nerve and produce optic atrophy in that eye, while the other eye develops papilledema from generalized elevation of pressure as the tumor expands in size, the Foster Kennedy syndrome. Other cardinal signs of brain tumor in addition to papilledema are persistent headache and vomiting. The headache is probably caused from the stretching of nerve endings in the dura mater. Irritation of the vagal nuclei in the floor of the fourth ventricle accounts for nausea and vomiting.

*Hydrocephalus* is an excessive accumulation of cerebrospinal fluid. Fluid sometimes collects in the subarachnoid space over the external surface of the brain following meningitis or trauma, but most cases of hydrocephalus are the result of blockage along the passageways and the extra fluid is in the ventricles of the brain. In *congenital hydrocephalus* an open path for cerebrospinal fluid fails to develop normally. Other developmental anomalies are also likely to be present. The head usually appears to be of normal size at birth, but it begins to show a disproportionate enlargement during the first few months. The thin skull, with its widely open sutures, offers little resistance to pressure from within and gradually swells to enormous proportions. Meanwhile the ventricles become greatly dilated and the brain substance is reduced to a thin shell. Obstructions of the cerebral aqueduct by an overgrowth of ependymal cells may prevent the passage of fluid from the third to the fourth ventricle, or a malformation of the medial and lateral apertures may block the outflow from the fourth ventricle. Frequently the stoppage is caused by an elongation of the medulla and cerebellum downward into the foramen magnum. This permits fluid to escape into the space around the spinal cord, but it cannot ascend to the basal cisterns above the foramen

126

magnum. In such cases a dye injected into one of the lateral ventricles can be recovered by needle puncture of the subarachnoid space in the lumbar region and the condition is known as *communicating hydro-cephalus.*

Samples of cerebrospinal fluid for diagnostic tests are obtained by directing a long needle between two upper lumbar vertebrae and insert-ing it far enough to reach and pierce the dura mater. There is no danger of injuring the nerve roots of the cauda equina which are present at this level. With the patient relaxed and in a recumbent position the pressure of the spinal fluid should not exceed 150 mm. of water. The pressure rises to about 300 mm. $H_2O$ with the patient in the sitting position. Small oscillations of the fluid level in a manometer connected to the needle arise from the transmission of the cerebral pulse. These pulsations indicate that free communication is present. If blockage of the spinal subarachnoid space is suspected, the *Queckenstedt test* can be performed. With the needle in place and a water manometer attached, the jugular veins are compressed for ten seconds. Under normal conditions there will be a rapid rise and fall in pressure, normal levels returning within fifteen seconds. This is a negative test. The test is positive if no change in pres-sure occurs. The test should never be performed if symptoms of elevated intracranial pressure are present because of the danger of cerebellar tonsil herniation. Even lumbar punctures should be performed cautiously in the presence of elevated intracranial pressure, since the release of pressure from below may allow similar herniation. If the medulla protruded into the foramen magnum, death could result from damage to the cardiac and respiratory centers.

Spinal fluid can also be obtained by passing a needle at the base of the skull directly through the atlanto-occipital membrane into the cisterna magna. No nervous structures are encountered, but the needle would strike the medulla if it should slip too far and, for this reason, cisternal puncture is not often attempted by inexperienced persons.

## Pneumoencephalography

If the pineal body is calcified, its shadow may be seen in x-rays and displacement in its position may give significant information. Thinning or erosion of skull bones, as shown by x-ray, may help to establish the presence of a mass in the adjacent parts of the brain. Most tumors, how-ever, cannot be visualized directly unless they are partly calcified. If the cerebrospinal fluid is completely withdrawn from the ventricular spaces and replaced by air, these spaces will appear as shadows in an x-ray. Dila-tions, distortions in shape, and filling defects can then be studied in con-siderable detail. This process—*pneumoencephalography*—is accomplished by means of lumbar puncture. If the intracranial pressure is increased, lumbar puncture cannot be performed safely and it is necessary to intro-duce air directly into the ventricular system to obtain a visible outline by x-ray—*ventriculography*. This process requires the drilling of trephine holes in the parietal bones through which needles can be passed into both lateral ventricles.

127

# Index

128

Body (bodies) (*continued*)
lateral geniculate, 35, 36, 84, 85, 86, 102, 104, 111
medial geniculate, 37, 44, 65, 66, 102, 104, 111
Herring, 98
juxtarestiform, 68
mammillary, 35, 96, 100, 101, 107, 108
Nissl's, 32
pineal, 37, 96, 105, 108
displacement of, 127
tumor of, 83
restiform. See *Peduncle, inferior cerebellar*.
trapezoid, 40, 65
Body image, 112
Brachium, 1
conjunctivum. See *Peduncle, superior cerebellar*.
of inferior colliculus, 66
pontis. See *Peduncle, middle cerebellar*.
Brain, 2, 3
Brain stem, 2, 3, 32-34
lesions of, 78-83
Broca's area, 113
Brodman's areas, 109
Brown-Sequard's syndrome, 30
Bundle, medial forebrain, 97, 98, 107

CALAMUS scriptorius, 34, 37
Calcarine fissure, 85, 111, 114
Capsule, internal, 9, 96, 102, 113, 114
Carotid body, 56
Carotid sinus, 56
Cauda equina, 4
Caudate nucleus. See *Nucleus, caudate*.
Center
ciliospinal, 92
respiratory, of medulla, 56, 57
vasomotor, of medulla, 56
Central canal of spinal cord, 35
Central gray substance, 35, 37, 38, 43
Central nervous system, 2, 16
Cerebellum, 2, 3, 17, 18, 68, 72-77, 122
anterior lobe of, 72
clinical signs of dysfunction of, 76
cortex of, 72
feed-back circuits through, 75
flocculonodular lobe of, 41, 68, 72
folia of, 72
hemispheres of, 72
nuclei of, 41
pathways to and from, 73
posterior lobe of, 72
primary sulcus of, 72

Cerebellum (*continued*)
synergistic function of, 73
vermis of, 41, 72
Cerebral aqueduct, 42, 43, 44, 124, 125
Cerebral cortex, 109-118
areas of:
auditory (area 41), 66, 111
auditory association, 111
Broca's, 113
Brodman's, 109
frontal association, 110
motor (area 4), 4, 7, 104, 110, 122
olfactory, 107
prefrontal, 104, 110
premotor (area 6), 7, 104, 110, 121, 122
sensory association, 111
sensory receptive, 111
somesthetic, 17, 18, 21, 104, 111
striate, 85
suppressor (area 4S), 110
visual, 85, 102, 115
visual association, 85, 111
Wernicke's, 113
layers of, 109
nerve cells of, 109
Cerebral peduncles. See *Crus cerebri*.
Cerebrospinal fluid, 124, 127
circulation of, 124, 125
formation of, 124
pressure of, 126
Cerebrum, 2, 3
lobes of:
frontal, 2, 7, 103, 104, 108, 114
limbic, 100
parietal, 3, 7, 18, 103, 104, 114, 115
occipital, 3, 84, 104, 114, 115
temporal, 3, 101, 104, 114, 115
pars opercularis, 3
pars orbitalis, 3
pars triangularis, 3
Chorda tympani, 52, 55
Chorea
Huntington's, 123
Sydenham's, 123
Choroid plexus, 34, 124
of fourth ventricle, 34, 124
of lateral ventricle, 124
of third ventricle, 96, 102, 124
Chromatolysis, 32
Chromatophilic substance, 32
Cisterna, 124, 125
Clark, column of, 17, 18
Clava, 34, 37
Clonus, 13
Cochlea, 64

129

130

Fibers (*continued*)
  olivocochlear, 66
  postganglionic, 54, 91
  preganglionic
    cranial, 54, 93
    sacral, 93
    thoracolumbar, 91
  proprioceptive, 16, 17, 18, 48
  reticulospinal, 56, 70
  suppressor, 14
  of taste sense, 52, 55
  thalamocortical, 2, 18, 20, 104
  trigeminothalamic, 62
Fibrillations in muscle, 13
Field (fields)
  Forel's, 120
  motor eye, 8, 110
  prerubral, 121
  of vision, 85
Fifth nerve. See *Nerve, trigeminal.*
"Fight or flight" phenomenon, 93
Filum terminale, 4, 5
Final common path, 10
Fissure
  anterior median, 4, 6, 34
  calcarine, 85, 111, 114
  hippocampal, 100
  lateral, 2, 3, 65
  medial longitudinal, 2
  parieto-occipital, 3
Flaccid paralysis. See *Paralysis, flaccid.*
Flocculus, 72
Foramen (foramina)
  interventricular, 96, 124, 125
  jugular, 51, 52
  magnum, 34, 51, 126
Forel, decussation of, 44
Forel's fields, 120
Fornix, 97, 100, 101, 107, 114
Foster-Kennedy's syndrome, 126
Fourth nerve. See *Nerve, trochlear.*
Foville's syndrome, 81
Fröhlich syndrome, 99
Funiculus
  anterior, 4, 6
  lateral, 4, 6, 18
  posterior, 4, 6, 18, 27
    signs of injury, 19, 30

GAMMA motoneuron, 12
Ganglion (ganglia), 1
  aorticorenal, 91
  basal, 96, 119
  celiac, 91
  cervical, 91
  ciliary, 58, 87, 93
  geniculate, 48, 52, 55
  hypogastric, 92

Ganglion (ganglia) (*continued*)
  inferior
    of glossopharyngeal nerve, 52
    of vagus nerve, 49, 52
  mesenteric
    inferior, 92
    superior, 91
  otic, 49, 55, 93
  parasympathetic, 54
  paravertebral, 91
  prevertebral, 91, 92
  pterygopalatine, 52, 54, 93
  semilunar, 20, 35, 48, 61
  spinal, 13, 16
  spiral, 49, 64
  stellate, 91
  submandibular, 49, 52, 55, 93
  superior
    of glossopharyngeal nerve, 52
    of vagus nerve, 49, 52
  terminal, 93
  vestibular, 68, 69
General paresis, 111
Geniculate body. See *Body, geniculate.*
Geniculo-calcarine tract. See *Tract, geniculo-calcarine.*
Gennari's line, 85
Genu, internal, of facial nerve, 40, 41
Gigantopyramidal cells, 7
Globus pallidus, 103, 114, 119, 120, 121
Glossopharyngeal nerve. See *Nerve, glossopharyngeal.*
Gnosis, 112
Gray matter, 1, 4
Gyrus, 2
  angular, 3, 113
  anterior transverse temporal, 65, 66, 102
  cinguli, 100, 101, 103, 104, 108
  cuneus, 85, 86
  frontal, 3
    inferior, 3, 113
    middle, 8
  of Heschl, 65, 66, 102
  hippocampal, 100
  isthmus, 101
  lingual, 85, 86
  parahippocampal, 101, 107
  postcentral, 3, 18, 25, 55, 62, 111
  precentral, 3, 7, 8, 74, 110
  subcallosal, 108
  supramarginal, 3, 112
  temporal
    inferior, 3
    middle, 3
    superior, 3, 112

Medial longitudinal fissure, 2
Medulla, 34-39
  cranial nerves of, 51-56
  external structure of, 34
  internal structure of, 35
  lesions of, 78, 79
  reticular formation of, 13, 35, 37,
    38, 122
  vasomotor center of, 56
Membrane
  basilar, 64
  tympanic, 64
  vestibular, 64
Memory, 112
Meniere's syndrome, 71
Meynert, decussation of, 44
Micturition, 94
Midbrain, 42, 44, 112
  basis pedunculi. See *Crus cerebri.*
  cranial nerves of, 58
  external structure of, 42
  internal structure of, 43, 44
  lesions of, 82, 83
  reticular formation of, 98
  tectum of, 43
  tegmentum of, 43
Millard-Gubler's syndrome, 80
Monoplegia, 14
Motion sickness, 71
Motoneuron (motoneurons)
  alpha, 12
  gamma, 12
  lesions of, 61, 74
Motor area, 4, 7, 104, 110, 122
Motor end-plate, 12
Multiple neuritis, 28
Muscle (muscles)
  fasciculations of, 13, 60
  fibrillations of, 13
  innervation of:
    buccinator, 60
    ciliary, of iris, 93
    dilator, of iris, 91
    of facial expression, 59
    genioglossus, 51
    levator palpebrae superioris, 59
    masseter, 60
    oblique, 58, 59
    orbicularis oculi, 59, 89
    of pharynx, 52, 53
    pterygoid, 60
    rectus, 58, 59
    of soft palate, 53
    sphincter, of iris, 93
    sternomastoid, 51
    temporalis, 60
    trapezius, 51
  tonus, 11

Mydriasis, 59
Myelin sheath, 1, 32

NEOCEREBELLUM, 41, 72
Nerve (nerves), 1
  abducent, 8, 35, 39, 40, 48, 58, 80
  accessory, spinal, 8, 34, 50, 51
    bulbar portion, 35, 36, 51, 53,
      54
    spinal portion, 35, 51
  acoustic, 35, 36, 39, 80, 81
    cochlear division, 64, 65
    vestibular division, 68, 69, 73
  chorda tympani, 52, 55
  cochlear, 64, 65
  facial, 8, 35, 36, 39, 40, 48, 59, 61,
    62, 80
    lower motor neuron lesion of, 59
    sensory and parasympathetic di-
      vision of, 51, 93
    supranuclear lesion of, 60
  functional components, 45, 50, 90
  glossopharyngeal, 8, 34, 35, 36, 49,
    52, 54, 55, 93
  hypoglossal, 8, 34, 35, 36, 38, 50,
    51, 79
  intermedius, 35, 36, 48, 51, 52, 54,
    55, 59
  laryngeal, 53
  oculomotor, 8, 35, 36, 42, 44, 47,
    58, 83, 86
    accessory, 48, 87, 88
  olfactory, 47, 106
  optic, 35, 36, 47, 84, 85
  pelvic splanchnic, 90, 94
  pudendal, 93, 94
  stato-acoustic, 49
  spinal accessory. See *Nerve, ac-*
    *cessory.*
  splanchnic, 91, 92, 93
  trigeminal, 8, 35, 36, 39, 42, 48,
    60, 62, 82
    mandibular, 52
    mesencephalic root of, 42
    motor division of, 60
    nuclei of. See *Nuclei of trigem-*
     *inal nerve.*
    sensory division of, 61
    spinal root of, 20, 21, 36, 62, 80
  trochlear, 8, 35, 36, 43, 48, 58
  vagus, 8, 34, 35, 36, 49, 54, 55, 79
    branches of, 53
    complex, 51-56
    distribution of, 53
    motor portion of, 53
    parasympathetic portion of, 54,
      93
    sensory ganglia of, 52

Nucleus (nuclei) (*continued*)
  of trochlear nerve, 43, 58
  tuberal, 97
  ventromedial, of hypothalamus, 97, 99
  vestibular group, 36, 41, 46, 49, 68, 122
    lateral, 40, 41, 68, 69
    medial, 38, 68, 69
    spinal, 38, 68, 69
    superior, 40, 68, 69
  zona incerta, 120
Nystagmus, 69, 70, 77

Obex, 34, 37
Occipital lobe. See *Cerebrum, occipital lobe.*
Occipitotectal fibers, 88
Oculomotor nerve. See *Nerve, oculomotor.*
Olfactory afferent fibers, 100
Olfactory nerve, 47, 106
Olfactory reflexes, rhinencephalon and, 106-108
Olive, 34, 35, 36
Optic chiasm, 35, 84, 85, 86, 96
Optic disc, 84, 126
Optic nerve, See *Nerve, optic.*
Optic radiation. See *Tract, geniculocalcarine.*
Optic reflexes, 87-90
Optic tract, 35, 42, 84, 85, 86, 102
Organ of Corti, 64, 66
Osmoreceptor, 98

Pain, 20, 24
  pathway for, 20
  perception of, 20
  radicular, 22, 30
  referred, 22, 23, 24
  reflexes, 24, 89
  visceral, 22
Palate, innervation of, 53, 55
Paleocerebellum, 41, 72
Pallidum. See *Globus pallidus.*
Palsy, Bell's, 60
Papez theory of emotion, 101
Papilledema, 126
Paralysis agitans, 122
Paralysis
  flaccid, 13, 28, 31, 110
  of lateral gaze, 81, 82
  spastic, 13, 30, 82, 110
  of upward gaze, 83
Paraplegia, 14, 70
Parasympathetic nervous system, 93
Paresis, 14
  general, 111
Paresthesia, 22, 30

Parietal lobe. See *Cerebrum, parietal lobe.*
Parieto-occipital fissure, 3
Parinaud's syndrome, 83
Parkinson's disease, 122
Past-pointing, 76
Pathway (pathways)
  auditory, 65
  cerebellar afferent and efferent, 73
  cortico-mammillary, 97
  cortico-ponto-cerebellar, 74
  dentatorubrospinal, 75
  dentato-thalamo-cortical, 75
  linking hypothalamus and cerebrum, 99, 100
  olfactohypothalamic, 97
  olfactory, 107
  pain and temperature, 20
  proprioception, 16
  sense of simple touch and, 25
  tactile discrimination and, 18
  vestibular, 68, 69
  visual, 84, 85
  voluntary motor, 7
Peduncle (peduncles), 1
  inferior cerebellar, 18, 34, 36, 37, 40, 68, 72, 79
  middle cerebellar, 36, 37, 39, 40, 42, 72, 74
  superior cerebellar, 18, 36, 37, 39, 41, 42, 44, 72, 74, 103, 104
    decussation of, 43, 75
  cerebral. See *Crus cerebri.*
Pelvic splanchnic nerve, 90, 94
Perforated substance
  anterior, 108, 117
  posterior, 96, 117
Peripheral nervous system, 2
Perlia, nucleus of, 88
Phantom limb, 112
Pia mater, 3, 125
Pineal body. See *Body, pineal.*
Pituitary gland. See *Hypophysis.*
Plexus
  cardiac, 91
  carotid, 91
  choroid. See *Choroid plexus.*
  hypogastric, 94
  myenteric, 93
Pneumoencephalography, 127
Poliomyelitis, 28
Polydipsia, 98
Polyuria, 98
Pons, 39-42
  basilar portion of, 39
  cranial nerves of, 58
  external structure of, 39

135